THE DEVIL'S HIGHWAY

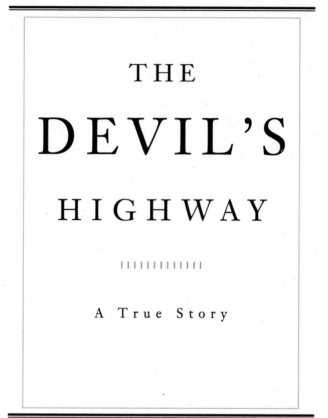

THE
DEVIL'S
HIGHWAY

||||||||||||

A True Story

LUIS ALBERTO URREA

LITTLE, BROWN AND COMPANY

New York   Boston

Little, Brown and Company
Time Warner Book Group
1271 Avenue of the Americas, New York, NY 10020
Visit our Web site at www.twbookmark.com

First Edition

Map by Jeffrey L. Ward

The author is grateful for permission to include lyrics from
"Bad Crazy Sun" by the Sidewinders. Words and music by
Rich Hopkins and David Slutes. Published by Magnificent
Amberson's Music/ Very Nearly Music/Careers Music, Inc./BMI.

Library of Congress Cataloging-in-Publication Data

Urrea, Luis Alberto.
The devil's highway : a true story / Luis Alberto Urrea.
p. cm.
Includes index.
ISBN 0-316-74671-1
1. Human smuggling—Mexican-American Border Region. 2. Illegal aliens—
Mexican-American Border Region—Crimes against. 3. United States—Emigration
and immigration—Social aspects. 4. Mexico—Emigration and immigration—
Social aspects. 5. Mexican-American Border Region—Social conditions. I. Title.

JV6475.U77 2004
304.8'73072—dc22
2003058930

10 9 8 7 6 5 4 3 2

Q-FF

Book design by Jo Anne Metsch

Printed in the United States of America

For the dead,
and for those who rescue
the living

Coyote's gone with most our money
And all our hope.
Left us just this side
Of Mexico.
Home feels like heaven
Compared to this.
I know the buzzards overhead
Hold salvation in their kiss.

It's this bad, crazy sun
That makes me think like that.

I lost my mind
And I lost my soul
And I know
That I'm never going home.

— THE SIDEWINDERS

CONTENTS

❘❘❘❘❘❘❘❘

AUTHOR'S NOTE

| | | | | | | |

This account was based on many sources. Interviews and travel, of course, provided many insights and testimonies. I was granted unusually generous access to documents and governmental reports from both Mexico and the United States; these were central to the collection of stories. Border Patrol reports, sheriff's department reports, Mexican consular reports, Justice Department reports, legal documents, testimonies and trial documents, correspondence, and many hours of taped interrogations and confessions went into the research. Due to concerns about the personal safety of the survivors, their actual depositions were sealed. I spent hours in federal defenders' offices, in various consulates, in Border Patrol stations, with Samaritan groups, in diners over cups of coffee, in Migra trucks, and on the Devil's Highway itself. At the time of this investigation, the survivors were material witnesses in a criminal case, and were also clients in the notorious civil suit against the United States; because of this, they were shielded from direct contact with me. The hours of their torment, however, were well documented, often in their own words. And the Mexican officials who handle their cases were forthcoming with information, sometimes offered surreptitiously, off the record, or representing messages the survivors wanted heard. Some of the sources for this book did not choose to be—or could not be—quoted directly.

The year I spent researching and traveling consumed four leather-bound notebooks of about 144 pages each. Much of that material, of course, was tangential. Still, about half of each notebook went into this book. Certain passages, nevertheless, were subject to educated conjecture. For example, no number of letters to Jesús Antonio Lopez Ramos, aka Mendez, will ever be answered. He simply won't answer questions, largely to protect his loved ones from payback by the Coyote gang. Fortunately, his testimony and writings and taped *pensées* are available for study. Any discussion of his private thoughts and motivations could only be taken on faith based on his various statements—some of them contradictory. The opinions of his attorney and of the Mexican officials who dealt with him were also of great help in decoding the cipher that is Mendez.

Furthermore, some conversations were implied—they are presented in the text as possibilities based on recollections and inferences from the recorded testimonies. These are shown without quotation marks. Where the actual words are known, they are presented as straight dialogue.

Finally, although I wasn't with them on the morning when they awoke lost in the Sonoran desert, I have spent many spring mornings there. I know the smell and sound of the dawn quite well. I know the time of year. And I know the weather conditions in which they found themselves. The Wellton 26 had scant time to worry about the nature aspects of their journey. But no story about death and the Devil's Highway could rightly exist without the strong presence of Desolation, in all its intimidating glory.

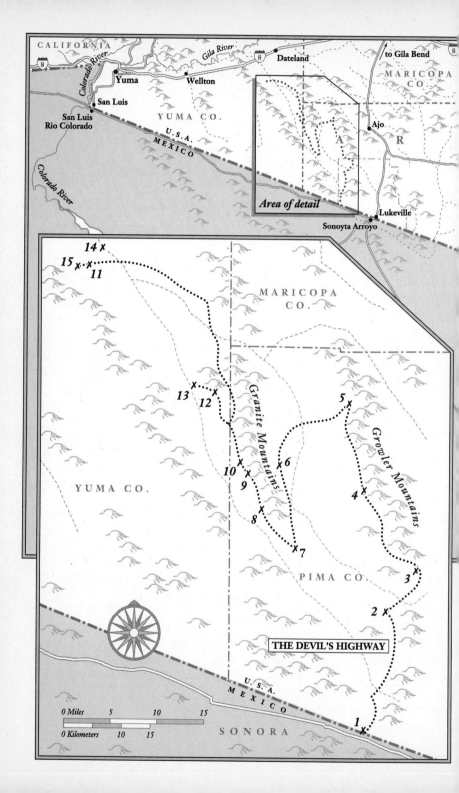

CALIFORNIA

Colorado River

Gila River

to Gila Bend

MARICOPA CO.

Dateland

Yuma

Wellton

San Luis

YUMA CO.

U.S.A.
MEXICO

San Luis Rio Colorado

Ajo

A   R

Colorado River

Area of detail

Lukeville

Sonoyta Arroyo

14 ✗
15 ✗ ✗
11

MARICOPA CO.

13 ✗ ✗
12

Granite Mountains

5 ✗

Growler Mountains

6 ✗

10 ✗
9 ✗

4 ✗

YUMA CO.

8 ✗

7 ✗

3 ✗

2 ✗

PIMA CO.

THE DEVIL'S HIGHWAY

U.S.A.
MEXICO

0 Miles   5   10   15

0 Kilometers   10   15

1 ✗

SONORA

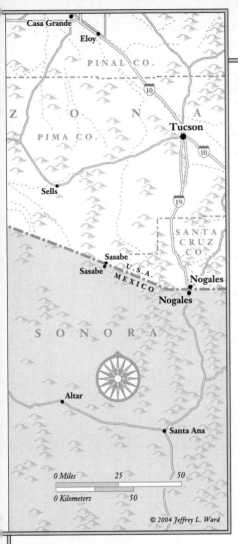

© 2004 Jeffrey L. Ward

1. Saturday, May 19, 1:40 p.m.
Group entered by vehicle at Quitobaquito.

2. Saturday, May 19, 3:00 p.m. High temp. 96°.
Group was dropped off at this location and told to follow the guides on foot.

3. Saturday, May 19, 11:30 p.m.
Group arrived at this point and observed lights that they believed to be a Border Patrol Agent in Bluebird Pass.

4. Sunday, May 20, 6:00 a.m.
Group continued northwest and attempted to cross over the Growler Mountains several times.

5. Sunday, May 20, 2:00 p.m.
At this point, the group decided to rest during the heat of the day. After resting until night, the guides were disoriented and began walking westbound away from Ajo.

6. Sunday, May 20, 9:00 p.m. High temp. 96°.
The group arrived at the Granite Mountains. By this time, they were out of water.

7. Monday, May 21, 6:00 a.m.
The two guides collected money from the group and said they were going to get water. They told the group to wait in this location and abandoned the group.

8. Monday, May 21, 2:00 p.m. High temp. 95°.
When the group realized that the guides were not coming back, they decided to continue on. The group was desperate and out of water.

9. Tuesday, May 22, 2:00 p.m. High temp. 108°.
Two members of the group became ill and died in this location during the day.

10. Tuesday, May 22, 11:00 p.m.
Other members of the group became ill in this location and five left to go for help.

11. Wednesday, May 23, 5:00 a.m.
The guides that had abandoned the group continued walking northwest, almost reaching Dateland, Arizona, before they were overcome by the heat.

12. Wednesday, May 23, 7:30 a.m.
One of the five who had left the group became ill and was left behind in this location.

13. Wednesday, May 23, 10:00 a.m.
High temp. 110°. Initial group of four was encountered by Wellton agent here as he was cutting the Vidrios Drag.

14. Thursday, May 24, 5:00 a.m.
Another member of the group was tracked to this location, where he was found deceased.

15. Thursday, May 24, 6:00 a.m.
Another member of the group was tracked to this location and found alive.

PART ONE

||||||||

CUTTING

THE

DRAG

1

||||||||

The Rules of the Game

Five men stumbled out of the mountain pass so sunstruck they didn't know their own names, couldn't remember where they'd come from, had forgotten how long they'd been lost. One of them wandered back up a peak. One of them was barefoot. They were burned nearly black, their lips huge and cracking, what paltry drool still available to them spuming from their mouths in a salty foam as they walked. Their eyes were cloudy with dust, almost too dry to blink up a tear. Their hair was hard and stiffened by old sweat, standing in crowns from their scalps, old sweat because their bodies were no longer sweating. They were drunk from having their brains baked in the pan, they were seeing God and devils, and they were dizzy from drinking their own urine, the poisons clogging their systems.

They were beyond rational thought. Visions of home fluttered through their minds. Soft green bushes, waterfalls, children, music. Butterflies the size of your hand. Leaves and beans of coffee plants burning through the morning mist as if lit from within.

Rivers. Not like this place where they'd gotten lost. Nothing soft here. This world of spikes and crags was as alien to them as if they'd suddenly awakened on Mars. They had seen cowboys cut open cacti to find water in the movies, but they didn't know what cactus among the many before them might hold some hope. Men tore their faces open chewing saguaros and prickly pears, leaving gutted plants that looked like animals had torn them apart with their claws. The green here was gray.

They were walking now for water, not salvation. Just a drink. They whispered it to each other as they staggered into parched pools of their own shadows, forever spilling downhill before them: *Just one drink, brothers. Water. Cold water!*

They walked west, though they didn't know it; they had no concept anymore of destination. The only direction they could manage was through the gap they stumbled across as they cut through the Granite Mountains of southern Arizona. Now canyons and arroyos shuffled them west, toward Yuma, though they didn't know where Yuma was and wouldn't have reached it if they did.

They came down out of the screaming sun and broke onto the rough plains of the Cabeza Prieta wilderness, at the south end of the United States Air Force's Barry Goldwater bombing range, where the sun recommenced its burning. Cutting through this region, and lending its name to the terrible landscape, was the Devil's Highway, more death, another desert. They were in a vast trickery of sand.

In many ancient religious texts, fallen angels were bound in chains and buried beneath a desert known only as Desolation. This could be the place.

In the distance, deceptive stands of mesquite trees must have looked like oases. Ten trees a quarter mile apart can look like a cool grove from a distance. In the western desert, twenty miles looks like ten. And ten miles can kill. There was still no water; there wasn't even any shade.

Black ironwood stumps writhed from the ground. Dead for

five hundred years, they had already been two thousand years old when they died. It was a forest of eldritch bones.

The men had cactus spines in their faces, their hands. There wasn't enough fluid left in them to bleed. They'd climbed peaks, hoping to find a town, or a river, had seen more landscape, and tumbled down the far side to keep walking. One of them said, "Too many damned rocks." *Pinches piedras*, he said. Damned heat. Damned sun.

Now, as they came out of the hills, they faced the plain and the far wall of the Gila Mountains. Mauve and yellow cliffs. A volcanic cone called Raven's Butte that was dark, as if a rain cloud were hovering over it. It looked as if you could find relief on its perpetually shadowy flanks, but that too was an illusion. Abandoned army tanks, preserved forever in the dry heat, stood in their path, a ghostly arrangement that must have seemed like another bad dream. Their full-sun 110-degree nightmare.

| | | | | | | | |

"The Devil's Highway" is a name that has set out to illuminate one notion: *bad medicine*.

The first white man known to die in the desert heat here did it on January 18, 1541.

Most assuredly, others had died before. As long as there have been people, there have been deaths in the western desert. When the Devil's Highway was a faint scratch of desert bighorn hoof marks, and the first hunters ran along it, someone died. But the brown and red men who ran the paths left no record outside of faded songs and rock paintings we still don't understand.

Desert spirits of a dark and mysterious nature have always traveled these trails. From the beginning, the highway has always lacked grace—those who worship desert gods know them to favor retribution over the tender dove of forgiveness. In Desolation, doves are at the bottom of the food chain. Tohono O'Odham poet Ofelia Zepeda has pointed out that rosaries and

Hail Marys don't work out here. "You need a new kind of prayers," she says, "to negotiate with this land."

The first time the sky and earth came together, Elder Brother, I'itoi, was born. He still resides in a windy cave overlooking the western desert, and he resents uninvited visitors. Mountains are called do'ags. In the side of one do'ag can be found the twin caves where the spirit of the evil witch, Ho'ok, hides. The coyote-spirit of the place is called Ban, and he works his wicked pranks in the big open spaces.

Everywhere, red shadows. Tiny men live underground, and they are known to the Yaqui Indians hereabouts as Surem. In the past, before the first white man died, Yuku, the devil, controlled all the corn until the crows stole it from him and let some of it slip so men could eat. Mexico's oldest hoodoo, La Llorona, the wailing ghost, has been heard rushing down nearby creek beds. And its newest hoodoo, the dreaded Chupacabras (the Goat Sucker), has been seen attacking animals, lurking in outhouses, and even jumping in bedroom windows to munch on sleeping children. An Apache witness said the Chupacabras was a whispering kangaroo. It said, "Come here." He swore it did.

The plants are noxious and spiked. Saguaros, nopales, the fiendish chollas. Each long cholla spike has a small barb, and they hook into the skin, and they catch in elbow creases and hook forearm and biceps together. Even the green mesquite trees have long thorns set just at eye level.

Much of the wildlife is nocturnal, and it creeps through the nights, poisonous and alien: the sidewinder, the rattlesnake, the scorpion, the giant centipede, the black widow, the tarantula, the brown recluse, the coral snake, the Gila monster. The kissing bug bites you and its poison makes the entire body erupt in red welts. Fungus drifts on the valley dust, and it sinks into the lungs and throbs to life. The millennium has added a further danger: all wild bees in southern Arizona, naturalists report, are now Africanized. As if the desert felt it hadn't made its point, it added killer bees.

Today, the ancient Hohokam have vanished, like the Anasazi, long gone in the north. Their etchings and ruins still dot the ground; unexplained radiating lines lead away from the center like ghost roads in the shape of a great star. Not all of these paths are ancient. Some of the lines have been made by the illegals, cutting across the waste to the far lights of Ajo, or Sells, or the Mohawk rest area on I-8. Others are old beyond dating, and no one knows where they lead. Footprints of long-dead cowboys are still there, wagon ruts and mule scuffs. And beneath these, the prints of the phantom Hohokam themselves.

In certain places, boulders form straight lines, arrayed along compass directions on the burning plains. Among these stones are old rock piles in the shapes of arrows. They were left by well-wishers in 1890, aiming at a *tinaja* (water hole) hidden among crags. Cairns that serve as mysterious signposts for messages long forgotten mix with ancient graves. Etchings made in the hardpan with feet or sticks form animals centuries old and only visible from the air. Some of these cairns have been put in place by Border Patrol signcutters (trackers), and they are often at the junction of two desert paths, but the cutters just smile when you ask what they mean. One more secret of Desolation.

When the white men came, they brought with them their mania for record keeping. They made their way across the land, subduing indigenous tribes, civilizing the frontier. Missionaries brought the gentle word of the Lamb. Cavalrymen bravely tamed the badlands, built military outposts, settlements, ranches, and towns. Cowboys rode like the wind. Gunslingers fell. The worst bandits you could imagine drank rotgut and shot sheriffs, yet lived on in popular mythology and became the subjects of popular songs and cheap fictions. Railroads followed, and the great cattle drives, and the dusty range wars, and the discovery of gold and silver. In the great north woods, lumberjacks collected the big trees. The Alamo. The Civil War took out countless citizens in its desperate upheaval.

Every Tijuana schoolkid knows it: it's the history of Mexico.

| | | | | | | |

If the North American continent was broad ("high, wide, and lonesome"), then Mexico was tall. High, narrow, and lonesome. Europeans conquering North America hustled west, where the open land lay. And the Europeans settling Mexico hustled north. Where the open land was.

Immigration, the drive northward, is a white phenomenon.

White Europeans conceived of and launched El Norte mania, just as white Europeans inhabiting the United States today bemoan it.

They started to complain after the Civil War. The first illegal immigrants to be hunted down in Desolation by the earliest form of the Border Patrol were Chinese. In the 1880s, American railroad barons needed cheap skilled labor to help "tame our continent." Mexico's Chinese hordes could be hired for cheap, yet they could earn more in the United States than in Mexico, even at cut rates. Jobs opened, word went out, the illegals came north.

Sound familiar?

Americans panicked at the "yellowing" of America. A force known as the Mounted Chinese Exclusionary Police took to the dusty wasteland. They chased the "coolies" and deported them.

And today?

Sinful frontier towns with bad reputations. Untamed mountain ranges, bears, lions, and wolves. Indians. A dangerous border. Inhabitants speak with a cowpoke twang, listen to country music, dance the two-step, favor cowboy hats, big belt buckles, and pickup trucks. That ain't Texas, it's Sonora.

January 18, 1541.

Sonoita (also known as Sonoyta) was perhaps not much more than sticks and mud, but it was a stopping point for a Spanish expedition in search of, what else, gold. Even in 1541, Sonoita was the unwilling host of killers and wanderers. The leader of this clanking Spaniard patrol was a firebrand known as Melchior Díaz. He didn't especially want to spend his holidays in the broiling dust of Sonoita, but he was deep into hostile territory. It was commonly believed that the natives of the Devil's Highway devoured human children. The Spaniards weren't planning on settling—spread the cross around, throw up a mission, and hit the road in search of better things.

Melchior Díaz was trying to reach the Sea of Cortez, lying between the Mexican mainland and Baja California. Perhaps he knew that ahead of him lay the most hellish stretch of land in the entire north. The dirt paths he rode his horse down on that day are now the paved and semipaved barrio lanes of modern Sonoita. Some of the hubcap-popping boulders in Sonoita's hillside alleys are the same rocks on which Melchior's horse's shoes struck sparks.

He died trying to kill a dog.

He probably didn't have anything against canines—his troop had dogs that they used to hunt down game and humans. But there were also the feral creatures that dashed in from the outskirts of the settlement to slaughter his sheep. Melchior Díaz kept his sheep in small brush corrals, attended by his Indian slaves. But the wild dogs had a way of sneaking off with lambs when nobody was looking.

And Melchior was cranky. He had spent his holidays far from home, among the savages, and even Tucson was only a small scattering of huts and lean-tos. He couldn't have been farther from Mexico City or Spain. Sonoita was the end of the world. A Christmas in this outpost did not inspire joy. Besides, conquistadores were notoriously short on joie de vivre.

Melchior rode well, and he rode well armed. He certainly carried a sword and a fighting dagger. He probably carried a har-quebus and a long metal-tipped lance, the M16 of the day.

Melchior was a strong man and a powerful fighter. In the nar-ratives of the Coronado expedition, we see him plying his trade: ". . . the horsemen began to overtake [the Indians] and the lances cut them down mercilessly . . . until not a man was to be seen."

This rout of natives serves as the preface to the story of death that begins with Melchior Díaz.

|||||||

We know that he was riding his horse down one of the settlement paths. We can project the smells swirling around him: horse, dirt, his own stink, chickens, smoke, dung. Not all that different from the smells of today.

He was approaching his sheep pen, perhaps where the Así Es Mi Tierra taco shop, or a Pemex station stands today. Melchior squinted ahead and—Damn it to hell!—those lazy slaves of his had allowed a dog to get in the pen!

Perro desgraciado!

No record states how Melchior entered the pen, but it doesn't seem likely he stopped to open a gate. Not Melchior. He jumped over the fence, and in jumping, somehow he bobbled his lance throw and missed the dog entirely. You can see the dog yipping and sidestepping and making tracks for the horizon, casting wounded looks over his shoulder. And here is where Melchior Díaz died.

The record states that Melchior, somehow, "passed over" the lance. Did he fall from the horse? No one knows, but the lance managed to penetrate his gut and rip him open.

The desert ground must have seemed terribly hard as he hit it. As Melchior died (it took twenty gruesome days) on his stinking cot, he burned and howled. Flies settled in his entrails. Maybe the very dog that killed him drew near to sniff the rich meaty scent. The fallen angels of Desolation came out of the Cabeza Prieta, folded their hands over him, and smiled.

The land had been haunted before Melchior died, and it remained haunted afterward; 150 years after his death, Catholic apparitions plagued the tribes. Various peoples had alarming encounters with meddlesome white women who flew above their heads. In the lands of the O'Odham, a white woman bearing a cross came drifting down the Devil's Highway itself. The warriors who saw her immediately did the only practical thing they could: they filled her with arrows. They said she refused to die. Kept on flying. Her story was written down in 1699, but the scribe who wrote this history tells us it had happened so long ago that the tribe had already forgotten her.

Fifty years after this Blessed Virgin UFO, a female prophet came out of the desert. She was known as *La Mujer Azul.* The Blue Woman. They filled her full of arrows, too. This time, she died.

Jesuits rolled in. They made the People as unhappy as the mysterious spirit-women, and Pimas raided the town to bludgeon its missionary to death. Angry Yumas by the Colorado River dragged a Jesuit out into the light and beat him to death.

It was the nineteenth century, however, that really got the modern era of death rolling.

The Yumas got stirred up again and massacred the evil scalp-hunting Glanton gang by the banks of the river in the mid 1840s. Then, in 1848–49, the California gold rush began. Mexicans weren't immune to the siren call of treasure. By now, the Cabeza Prieta/Devil's Highway had been trod by white men and mestizos for 307 years. It was still little more than a rough dirt trail—it is still a rough dirt trail—but it was slyly posing as a handy southern route through Arizona. White Arizonans and Texans hove to and dragged their wagons. Thousands of travelers went into the desert, and piles of human bones revealed where many of them fell. Though the bones are gone, wagon ruts can still be found, and near these ruts, piles of stone still hide the remains of those who fell.

One writer who has focused on this desert, Craig Childs, tells of a pair of old bullet casings found out there. They were jammed together, and when pried apart, an aged curl of paper fell out. On the paper, someone had written, "Was it worth it?"

| | | | | | | |

The Sand Papagos saw the endless lines of scraggly Mexicans as a rolling supermarket. Their strategy was similar to their approach to the floating virgin: shoot arrows. Wagon train after wagon train was slaughtered. Besieged Mexicans begged their own army to protect them, but the Sand Papagos and their leader, a warrior named Quelele, the Carrion-Hawk, were ready for them, too.

Just to make sure the Mexicans got the point, Quelele let it be known that his favorite snack was dead Mexican. "I don't need the wagons!" he boasted. "Bring on the Mexican army! I am the Carrion-Hawk! I'm hungry for Mexican meat!"

Between Quelele and the harsh landscape, the numbers of dead soared beyond counting. Human skeletons were found lying beside the road, and eerie cattle and horses, reduced to blanched mummies, were reported to be standing out among the ironwood trees. Graves surrounded some waterholes, up to twenty-seven around one pothole alone.

A westerner named Francisco Salazar seems to have been the first to keep an eyewitness record of this phase of the killing fields. By 1850, he wrote, the Devil's Highway was "... a vast graveyard of unknown dead ... the scattered bones of human beings slowly turning to dust ... the dead were left where they were to be sepulchered by the fearful sand storms that sweep at times over the desolate waste."

In the following years, over four hundred people died of heat, thirst, and misadventure. It became known as the most terrible place in the world.

And it's beautiful. Edward Abbey, the celebrated iconoclast

and writer, loved the place. He chose to be buried there, illegally, among the illegal Mexicans he despised.

|||||||

A young Tucson man stops at a table in a Mexican restaurant and addresses the gathered eaters. He has overheard their conversation about the desert. He pulls up a chair and launches into his tale.

He is a warlock-in-training, studying with one of the many shamans plying their trade in the area. He smiles and confesses that a certain aspect of Tucson is bothering him. That empty dirt lot? Over on the corner of Fourth and Speedway? Like, a couple blocks from the Yokohama Rice Bowl?

The master has shown him that the lot has always been vacant, empty since the 1600s. Nobody has ever dared build upon it, and the houses around the lot are plagued by ghosts and poltergeists. But they're not really ghosts. Dude, they're demons. It's one of the seven open gates of hell. A magus can sit in his pickup and summon the Beast while eating a teriyaki bowl and Diet Coke.

Thus, this small narrative is also about Tucson, the civilized part of Desolation, a city with its own secrets and holes. A desert can be a scrape of land or a small gravel lot. You can imagine the spirit of the empty places. The places named for the devil himself.

|||||||

Route 86 begins its life in Tucson as "Ajo Way." Here, a source close to this story once saw the actual Cabeza Prieta.

Beyond the O'Odham village of Sells, near the Coyote (human-smuggler) pickup point of mile marker 27, there is a dirt bank beside Highway 86. A few concrete houses sit behind it, about one hundred yards from the road. On the top of the bank is a single mailbox, on a crooked white pole.

It wasn't even at night when the Cabeza Prieta showed itself. It wasn't dawn, or the gloaming of sunset. It was in the heart of a brutal desert afternoon. The sun was bright, and the temperatures were hovering at about 104. Not a cloud in sight.

Suddenly, the ground split. Just a little hole, more of a slit, really. Maybe an ant hill, gravel scattered around the edge. Dirt welling up out of the hole like water.

Out of the small hole rose a black human head. It glistened, either wet or made of coal, some black crystal. Its eyes were burning white. Its teeth were also white. Its face was narrow, and it sported a sharp beard on its chin. It rose until just the tops of its shoulders were visible. It cast a shadow. And it turned as it watched the traveler pass.

It was laughing at him.

| | | | | | | |

The men walked onto the end of a dirt road. They couldn't know it was called the Vidrios Drag. Now they had a choice. Cross the road and stagger along the front range of the mountains, or stay on the road and hope the Border Patrol would find them. The Border Patrol! Their nemesis. They'd walked into hell trying to escape the Border Patrol, and now they were praying to get caught.

In their state, a single idea was too complex, and they looked upon it with uncertainty. They shuffled around. It was ten o'clock in the morning, 104 degrees. Dust devils, dead creosote rattling like diamondbacks, the taunting icy chip of sunlight reflected off a high-flying plane. Weird sounds in the landscape: voices, coughs, laughter, engines. It was the desert haunting they'd been hearing all along. When they heard the engine coming, it sounded like locusts flying overhead, cicadas, wind. And the dust rising could have been smoke from small fires. The flashes of white out there, heading toward them, popping out from behind saguaros and paloverde trees—well, it could have been ghosts, flags, a parade. It could have been anything. They didn't know if they should hide or stand their ground and face whatever was coming their way.

When the windshield flashed in the morning sun, they stood, they walked, ran, tripped, fell. Toward the truck, the white truck. The unlikely geometry of disaster once again worked them into its eternal ciphers.

Border Patrol agent Mike F., at the tail end of another dull drag, was driving his Explorer at a leisurely pace. No fresh sign anywhere on the ground. Boredom. He was about to pull a U and head back to 25E, the dirt road that cut down from Interstate 8 to the Devil's Highway and the Mexican border beyond, looked up, and beheld the men as they walked out of the light. Nothing special. You got lost walkers all the time, people begging for a drink. They often gave themselves up when they realized the western desert had gotten the better of them. Sometimes, you beat them down with your baton, and sometimes everybody just laughed and drank your water.

Only one of the walkers stepped forward. The rest hid under trees. They were watching Mike F. like deer in the shadows.

He took in the scene as he rolled toward them.

He stopped, put the truck in park, and opened his door. He put out a foot and gestured for them with one hand to stay put while he got the radio mike with the other and called in to Wellton Station. Cops tend to assess a situation at first glance—people are always up to something. In the desert, they were often involved in some form of dying. Most of them, if not in trouble, were sneaky. If they weren't illegals, or smugglers, or narco mules, they were trespassing on the military base in some Ed Abbey desert fantasy, or they were cactus thieves, swiping young saguaros for their Scottsdale gardens. Gringos caused more alarm out there than Mexicans. And the OTMs—Other Than Mexicans—were so hapless and weird that you'd just laugh. Like the time they found a large group of Arabs in matching slacks and neckties, like some demented terrorist Jehovah's Witness neighborhood canvass. "Oh? Are we here illegally? Oh! This is, you say, the United States? Right here? No, we did not know that. Praise to God. We were taking a walk, *Allahu Akbar*."

Bad guys had cornered the market on trying to look casual and "innocent." Mexicans, when not giving up, when not running like maniacs, often got wide-eyed, like a two-year-old stealing cookies. I didn't do nothin'! I was just out here looking around! The more innocent they acted, the more nervously slouchy and devil-may-care or childlike in their sinlessness, the more hinky the whole scene was, and the cop would start fingering his sidearm.

These guys were clearly no threat—no need to unholster a weapon yet. The radio call went something like: "We've got five bodies on Vidrios Drag, over." His voice probably sounded bored.

"Getting bodies," in Border Patrol lingo, didn't necessarily mean collecting corpses. Bodies were living people. "Bodies" was one of the many names for them. Illegal aliens, dying of thirst more often than not, are called "wets" by agents. "Five wets" might have slipped out. "Wets" are also called "tonks," but the Border Patrol tries hard to keep that bon mot from civilians. It's a nasty habit in the ranks. Only a fellow border cop could appreciate the humor of calling people a name based on the stark sound of a flashlight breaking over a human head.

Agent F. did not say he had "tonks" on the road.

Arrests of illegals are often slightly wry, vaguely embarrassing events. The relentless border war is often seen as a highly competitive game that can even be friendly when it's not frightening and deadly. Agents often know their clients, having apprehended them several times already. Daytime arrests have a whole different tone than lone midnight busts, out there in an abandoned landscape where the nearest backup might be a hundred hard miles away. But night or day, the procedure tends to be the same. The cop gets out of the truck and adjusts his gunbelt and puts his hands on his hips and addresses the group in

Spanish: "Hola, amigos! Estan arrestados." The Border Patrol so terrifies some of them that they give up immediately. Things happen. Stories burn all along the borderlands of Border Patrol men taking prisoners out into the wasteland and having their way with them. Women handcuffed, then groped and molested. Coyotes shot in the head.

Texas Rangers allegedly handcuff homeboys and toss them into irrigation canals to drown, though the walkers can't tell the Border Patrol apart from the Rangers or any other mechanized hunt squad: they're all cowboys. Truncheons. Beatings. Shootings. Broken legs. Torn panties. Blood. Tear gas. Pepper spray. Kicked ribs. Rape. These are the words handed from border town to border town, a savage gospel of the crossing. And the dark image of the evil Border Patrol agent dogs every signcutter who goes into the desert in his truck. It's the tawdry legacy of the human hunt—ill will on all sides. Paranoia. Dread. Loathing. Mexican-American Border Patrol agents are feared even more by the illegals than the gringos, for the Mexicans can only ascribe to them a kind of rabid self-hatred. Still, when the walkers are dying, they pray to be found by the Boys in Green.

The Border Patrol is understandably touchy about this reputation. They think the Jack Nicholson film *The Border*, where all agents and officers are corrupt, is funny as hell. They recommend a good Charles Bronson film about the Border Patrol if you want to know what it's really like. Something a little more straight up, more cowboy — cowboy in a good way, in the traditional way.

The five men rushed toward the truck.

"They're dying," they gasped.

"Who's dying?"

"Men. Back there. Amigos."

Seventeen men, they said.

Agent F. gave them water. They gulped. They puked the water back out and didn't care. They drank more.

"Muertos! Muertos!"

Seventeen. Then thirty. One man thought there were seventy bodies fallen behind them.

When Agent F. called it in to Wellton, the station's supervisory officer said, "Oh, shit."

For a long time, the Border Patrol had worried that something bad was coming. Something to match or outstrip the terrible day in 1980 when a group of Salvadorans was abandoned in Organ Pipe Cactus National Monument, and thirteen of them died. If it was the Border Patrol's job to apprehend lawbreakers, it was equally their duty to save the lost and the dying.

The guys at Wellton knew the apocalypse had finally come.

| | | | | | | | |

Southern Arizona is divided into two Border Patrol sectors, Tucson and Yuma. Fifteen hundred agents patrol Tucson sector; three hundred work Yuma. Tucson handles the eastern half of the state, starting at the small city of Ajo and covering Tucson, Nogales, Douglas, Patagonia, and so on. Yuma sector patrols the west, all the way to the Colorado River and beyond. They are responsible for Gila Bend, Dateland, Wellton, San Luis, and Yuma. Strangely enough, they also patrol into California's Imperial County. This has caused legal tribulations with the Mexican consulate in Calexico, California: illegals apprehended in eastern California should be tried in San Diego, but they are transported to Phoenix, where their cases are heard. Responsibility for these people can stretch from San Diego to Calexico to Tucson and finally to Phoenix. It only adds to the general chaos that rules the border, a chaos that the Tucson consul calls "the politics of stupidity."

Both Border Patrol sectors had been hammered by growing tidal waves of illegals. Urban crossings had been sealed off, and now smaller rural crossings were systematically clamping down. Operation Gatekeeper, the final solution to the border crossings, introduced by California in the late nineties, had ushered in a new era of secure urban borders and trampled wilderness. San Diego, Calexico, Yuma, El Paso, Nogales, Douglas, they were all becoming harder to get through. This looked great for the politicians of the cities. Voila! No more Mexicans!

Bigger fences, floodlights, a Border Patrol truck every half-mile, sensors, infrared spy videos, night vision cameras, Immigration and Naturalization Service checkpoints on all major freeways in and out of town, more agents.

But now, smaller, rougher places were becoming hot spots. The drug-smuggling village of Naco, for example. The small chicken-scratch settlement of Sasabe. The Tohono O'Odham reservation's small villes.

And astounding numbers of humans were moving through their deserts. Organ Pipe Cactus National Monument, a relatively compact portion of Tucson sector, was withering under two hundred thousand walkers passing through every year. Deaths were on the rise: in the half decade before Mike F. found the five walkers on Vidrios Drag, more than two thousand people had died along the Mexican border. Death by sunlight, hyperthermia, was the main culprit. But illegals drowned, froze, committed suicide, were murdered, were hit by trains and trucks, were bitten by rattlesnakes, had heart attacks.

The unofficial policy was to let them lie where they were found, resting in peace where they fell. Any fan of Joseph Wambaugh books or cop shows on TV can figure out the rest of the story. All cases, for all cops, require paperwork. The Border Patrol is no different. Each corpse generates a case file. Every unidentified corpse represents one case forever left open—you can never close the case if you can never find out who the dead walker was or where he or she came from. But uncollected—unreported—bones generate no files. Besides, how do the agents know if the bones are one hundred years old?

The Arizona Border Patrol's beat included this deadly western desert, a region enclosing Organ Pipe and the Cabeza Prieta wilderness, the Papago (Tohono O'Odham) reservation, the northern fingers of the Mexican Pinacate desert, the Goldwater bombing range, and the dreaded Camino del Diablo—the Devil's Highway. It is a vast trapezoid of land, bound by I-19 to the east, and the Colorado River to the west; I-8 to the north, and Mexican Route 2 and the imaginary border to the south.

I I I I I I I I

You'd be hard pressed to meet a Border Patrol agent in either southern Arizona sector who had not encountered death. It would be safe to say that every one of them, except for the rankest probie just out of the academy, had handled at least one dead body. And they all knew the locations of unidentified skeletons and skulls. Bones peppered the entire region.

All the agents seem to agree that the worst deaths are the young women and the children. Pregnant women with dying fetuses within them are not uncommon; young mothers have been found dead with infants attached to their breasts, still trying to nurse. A mother staggers into a desert village carrying the limp body of her son; doors are locked in her face. The deaths, however, that fill the agents with deepest rage are the deaths of illegals lured into the wasteland and then abandoned by their Coyotes. When the five dying men told Agent F. they'd been abandoned, he called in the information.

The dispatcher responded with a Banzai Run.

I I I I I I I I

The town of Wellton is in a wide plain on I-8. It is tucked between Yuma's mountain ranges and the Mohawk Valley, with its strange volcanic upthrusts. The American Canal cuts through the area, and a bombing range is to the south. Running just below I-8 is the railway line that carries freight from Texas to California. Most train crews have learned to carry stores of bottled water to drop out of their locomotives at the feet of staggering illegals.

Wellton Station sits atop a small hill north of the freeway. It is isolated enough that some car radios can't pick up a signal on either AM or FM bands. Cell phones often show "Out of Service Area" messages and go mute.

Many agents, borderwide, commute a fair distance to their stations. Drives of twenty, forty, even seventy miles are common. But the trips to and from work afford them a period of quiet, of wind-down or wind-up time. It is not always easy to leap from bed and go hunt people. Besides, the old-timers have learned to really love the desert, the colors in the cliffs, the swoop of a red-tailed hawk, the saffron dust devils lurching into the hills.

For most agents, it works this way: you get up at dawn and put on your forest green uniform. As you get to work, you pull in behind the station to the fenced lot. You punch in your code on the keypad, and you park beside the other machines safe from your enemies behind the chain-link. Your station is a small Fort Apache. On one side, the agents line up their trucks and sports cars, and on the other side sits the fleet of impeccably maintained Ford Explorers. Border Patrol agents are often military men, and they are spit-and-polish. Their trucks are clean and new; their uniforms are sharp; and their offices are busy but generally squared away. The holding cells in the main building—black steel mesh to the far left of the main door—sparkle. Part of this is, no doubt, due to the relentless public focus on the agency. In Calexico, the Mexican consulate has upped the ante by placing a consulate office inside the actual station: prisoners are greeted by the astounding sight of a service window with Mexican flags and Mexican government signs.

Inside, Wellton Station is a strange mix of rundown police precinct and high-tech command center. Old wood paneling, weathered tables. Computers and expensive radios at each workstation. In the back building, supervisory officer and mainstay of the station Kenny Smith has a couple of radios going, which he listens to, and a couple of phones ringing every few minutes, which he generally ignores. A framed picture of a human skull lying in the desert hangs on the wall. It has a neat hole in the forehead, above one eye socket. "Don't get any cute ideas," one of the boys says. "We didn't shoot that guy."

A computer is on all the time, and GPS satellite hardware bleeps beside it. Above Kenny's desk is a huge topo map showing the region. He sits in a swivel chair and reigns over his domain. He has an arrow with its notched end stuffed into a gas station antenna ball. He holds the ball in his fist and uses the arrow to point out various things of interest on the map.

On the wall is the big call-chart. Names and desert vectors are inked onto a white board in a neat grid. Agents' last names are linked to their patrol areas. In the morning, you check the board, banter with Kenny, say good morning to the station chief, stop by to say hello to Miss Anne, who runs the whole shebang from her neat desk in the big main room out front.

The town of Wellton is farms and dirt, dirt and farms. New agents, fresh from the East or West coasts, amuse the old boys by asking where they can find an espresso or a latte. Kenny Smith tells them, "Well, you can go down to Circle K and get a sixteen-ounce coffee. Then put some flavored creamer in it." That one never fails to get a laugh out of the old boys. An agent, sipping his stout coffee, is mid-story: ". . . And here comes Old José," he says, "all armed-up on some girlie!" Old José seems to be the archetypal tonk who shows up in stories. The listener, a steroidal-looking Aryan monster with a military haircut and a bass voice, notes: "Brutal." He turns to his computer keyboard and plugs away with giant fingers.

Everybody speaks Spanish. Several of the agents are Mexican Americans. Quite a few in each sector who aren't "Hispanic" are married to Mexican women.

Wellton Station is considered a good place to work. The old boys there are plain-spoken and politically incorrect. INS and Border Patrol ranks are overrun with smooth-talking college boys mouthing carefully worded sound bites. Not so in Wellton. Agents will tell you that the only way to get a clear picture of the real border world is to find someone who has been in service over four years. A ten-year veteran is even better. Wellton has its share of such veterans, but any agent who has been in service for ten years knows better than to talk to you about his business.

A great compliment in the Border Patrol is: "He's a good guy." Wellton's agents are universally acknowledged by other agents as good guys. Jerome Wofford, they say, will give you the shirt off his back; the station chief will lend you his cherry SUV if you have special business.

Like the other old boys of Wellton Station, you love your country, you love your job, and though you would never admit it, you love your fellow officers. Civilians? They'll just call you jack-booted thugs, say you're doing a bad job, confuse you with INS border guards. You're not a border guard, you're a beat cop. Your station chief urges you not to hang out in small-town restaurants, not to frequent bars. Don't go out in uniform. Don't cross the border. Don't flash your badge. Don't speed, and if you do and get tagged for a ticket, don't use your badge to try to get out of it. Don't talk to strangers. In hamlets like Naco, San Luis, Nogales, civilians often won't make eye contact. Chicanos don't like you. Liberals don't like you. Conservatives mock and insult you. And politicians . . . politicians are the enemy.

There's always someone working in the office, early or late, every day and every night of every year. They're guarding the cells, monitoring the radios, writing reports. Sometimes, you can't sleep. You can always come in to the clubhouse and find someone to talk to. Somebody who votes like you, talks like you. Believes in Christ or the Raiders like you. You can make coffee for the illegals in the cage, flirt with the señoritas—though with all the sexual assault and rape charges that dog the entire border, you probably don't. Human rights groups are constantly lodging complaints, so you watch yourself. The tonks supposedly have phones in their holding pens so they can call lawyers to come slaughter you if you do anything wicked. You pull up one of the rolling office chairs, turn your back to them, and sit at a radio and listen to the ghostly voices of your partners out in the desert night, another American evening passing by.

|||||||||

But that's later. Now you get your assignment and you head out. You're usually alone. You pick up your vehicle from the yard. The station has its own gas pump, so you use your government card and fill the tank. You have a thermal jug of cool water. Sometimes you have a military map tube with topo maps. You have a GPS unit, and a radio on your belt. You have cuffs, pepper spray, and a baton. You carry a .40 caliber sidearm in a holster at your hip. It has a clip loaded with hollow-point rounds. "You shoot a guy to kill him, not to hurt him." That's the mantra. You carry extra clips.

The Explorers are nice. You go out there four-wheeling in an SUV that has been retrofitted by felons in a Texas prison. (Ain't that rich. The only thing you think would be richer would be if illegals in some Ford plant in Ohio fitted out your rig.) The Explorer has a cage behind the back seat, and a mounted radio down between the front seats, and a shotgun rack behind your seat, but separated from the wets by heavy mesh. An upright pump is usually clipped into the rack. They designed the truck without asking you. For a while there, they put radios in the trucks with the mike on the opposite side from the driver. You had to lean over the whole unit and feel around on the passenger's side. And some genius has designed the shotgun rack to go on the far side of the back seat, over by the door, so by the time you've bent back and struggled with it, the bad guy has busted caps in you. As it is, the mike on the radio is now exactly level with your right knee, so if you're not careful, you'll lean into it and punch the button and either jam the entire channel or transmit your own singing, farting, talking to yourself. The trucks weigh ten thousand pounds, so even in four wheel drive you can hit a sand pit and sink. You come out of that little crisis covered in dust like flour, looking like a ghost, and the assholes back at the station just about fall down laughing.

If they'd just let the beat cops run the asylum, you think, a lot of things would change.

The trucks have two standard features that everyone finds indispensable: a killer AC unit and a strong FM radio. With ground temperatures soaring to 130 on sunny days, and on certain nights dropping only as low as 98, the air conditioner is a lifesaver—literally. You can cool down a burning body right quick with the AC blasting, and with AC and a water jug, you can keep an illegal alive until the BORSTAR (Border Patrol Search, Trauma and Rescue) lifesavers swoop in with their helicopters. They're the Border Patrol's Air Cav. Cute red T-shirts. You save the wets and the boys in red fly in and get all the glory. You crap behind a bush, trying to keep it off your shoes, but BORSTAR goes on ABC nightly news.

As for the FM . . . driving 150 miles at thirty miles an hour, alone, scanning the ground for sign, is boring. Even the night runs, once your probie nerves wear off, are boring. Old boys try to liven them up for you. When you're new, they tell you the Chupacabras is out there on Vidrios Drag, and he sucks blood from lone wanderers. Or Bigfoot's been seen coming out of the Tinajas Altas pass. Or there are ghosts of dead walkers creeping around the Camino del Diablo. Sometimes the bastards will even sneak up on you and shout, right around 3:00 A.M. when you're sleepy, but that's a good way to get shot, so most of them don't bother. The FM keeps morale elevated. Radio calls to base often have a classic rock soundtrack—Van Halen and Led Zeppelin bleed through the call-ins. Sometimes, newbies will be blasting the radio so loud they can't hear calls from dispatch.

"Ten, base, ten. I'm twentied at the Pinacate Lava Flow. I'M GONNA GIVE YOU EVERY INCH OF MY LOVE! Over."

One nonstandard lifesaver fits into the space between the base radio and the passenger seat. A roll of toilet paper. It beats a handful of cactus.

||||||||

You grab a coffee at Circle K, microwave a burrito, then cross I-8 on the old bridge and head south on 25E. To the west, 29E parallels you. It is the actual terminus of the Devil's Highway. The twin E's take you to the Mexican border, crossing miles of a sere and mysterious bombing range. Your ironist's eye loves to pick out crazy things. Right near the Devil's Highway itself is a mutated saguaro that rises ten feet into the sky. Its main body is thick, and the top is a scarred, messed-up ball of tissue. It looks for all the world like an arm raising a fist. And wouldn't you know it, the "ears," or branches, that stick out form an index finger and a little finger. The Devil's Highway throws up a heavy metal devil sign to announce itself. The only thing missing is Ozzy Osbourne.

The aforementioned Army tanks molder in the eastern end of the basin. When no one is around (and no one is ever around) you can shoot at them for fun. On the west end, under Raven's Butte, there's an abandoned squadron of jet fighters. Rounds penetrate their skin easily. (You can't hardly even chip the paint off the tanks, though.) Sometimes, jet jockeys target the Border Patrol trucks and dog them from on high, vectoring in on their white roofs. Many of the Wellton guys enjoy flipping them the bird out the window, or even jumping from the truck in the middle of the faux strafing run and raising the finger at the startled pilots.

Marine patrols training on the dirt roads interdict the sign-cutters. It's pure bullshit—pulling an agent over at gunpoint and demanding papers. This is supposed to be America. And how dumb do the jarheads have to be to pull over a federal agent, in uniform, in a clearly marked patrol car?

The sign announcing the advent of the Devil's Highway has been liberally punctuated by .50 caliber machine gun rounds. Those bored jarheads again. If you're out early, you'll see snakes on the road, soaking up some heat. Sidewinders are fun to harass—you can pull up next to them and pour water on their heads. They have fits, but don't know who to bite. It's a riot.

There are other games the Border Patrol guys play. Sometimes they toss a recently shot rattlesnake, dead but still writhing and rattling, into the cage with the captured wets. Ha ha—that's a funny sight, watching them go apeshit in the back of the truck. And they get it, right? Old José has a good sense of humor about it. He pissed his pants and screamed at first, but then he laughed and called the agent "Pinche Migra!" and swear to God, he peeled that snake right there and ate it!

An agent out of Wellton once pulled a classic practical joke on his load of clients out near 25E. One of his boys had been taking potshots in the desert, and he'd plugged a jackrabbit. "Hey," the agent told him, "I've got an idea." He took the big jack and tucked it into some bushes near the road.

Later in the day, he had some Mexicans in the back, and he was tooling along, taking them back to the station holding pens.

Suddenly, he stopped the car and said, "Muchachos, un conejo!" A rabbit!

They crowded the front of the cage and said, "Donde?"

"Allí, allí. Mira. Es grande!"

They squinted and frowned, but nobody saw no stinking rabbit.

"Right there, man!" the agent cried.

A vast plain of saguaro and dry brush and ironwood stumps.

"I'm going to shoot it," he told them. "I'll show you how good the Migra is with our *pistolas*."

He hopped out of the truck and squeezed off a shot with his pistol.

"*Chinga'o!* He's shooting!" They flinched. Ducked. He holstered his weapon and got in the truck.

"Got him!" he said. "Let's go see."

He drove—they thought it was fifty yards, maybe. But he drove past that. And then he drove a mile. They were muttering and whistling. Then another mile. Then another damn mile. He pulled up to the saguaro cluster where he'd stashed the carcass, parked again, jumped out and dug the rabbit out of the bushes. He held it up so they could see it.

They cried out in shock and awe.

"I told you the Migra were good shots!" he told them.

The guys at the station laughed for years about that one.

I I I I I I I I

Drags are created by bundles of five car tires attached to a frame, looking somewhat like the Olympic rings. Every few days, a truck chains a drag to its back end and drives the roads, ironing the sand into a smooth surface. The drags tend to cut east/west. Since the illegals head north, they are forced, sooner or later, to cross a drag. The Devil's Highway itself is the Mother of All Drags.

The fiendish ploys of the Coyotes offer you many opportunities to hone your signcutting skills. The whole game for their team is to pass by invisibly, and the team on this side is paid to see the invisible. The Coyotes score when they make it, and the Migra scores when they don't. Like pro wrestling, there is a masked invader who regularly storms the field to disrupt the game. This, of course, is La Muerte.

The illegals try to leap across the drags, but the drags are often wide enough to make jumpers hit the ground at least once. They walk backward, hoping to confuse cutters. You have to be good to confuse a veteran. An Indian reservation cop says, "Them trackers can probably tell you what color the guy's hair was, and that he had eighty-nine cents in his left pocket. Then they can tell you the last time he got laid."

Lately, foamers have been walking the desert. Foamers tape blocks of foam rubber to their feet, thus leaving no prints. Or so they think. Foam blocks make small right-angle dents in the soil at their corners. And sooner or later, the heel of the walker will wear through the foam, and the cutter can see a weird pattern, like a small half-moon hoof in a picture frame. Your classic foamer sign.

Every Coyote team relies on the old Apache trick of the brush-out. Last man through walks backward, brushing the tracks away with a branch of some bush. It's such a standard move that Border Patrol agents call giving civilians and media types evasive answers a brush-out. The Washington, D.C., desk jockeys are considered the ultimate brush-out masters.

There is room, in this desert world, for scholarship as well as sport.

Cutters read the land like a text. They search the manuscript of the ground for irregularities in its narration. They know the plots and the images by heart. They can see where the punctuation goes. They are landscape grammarians, got the Ph.D. in reading dirt.

On lava, a displaced stone will reveal a semicircle of lighter ground underneath. Likewise a pebble kicked out of place on the hardpan, where the desert varnish that accumulates on the ground reveals a crescent of paler sand. In-ground sensors are buried in places known only to the Border Patrol. These sensors are known as Oscars. A Coyote would give his teeth to get hold of this information.

Sometimes, the sensors are very cleverly placed—their little antennas stick up in the middle of creosote bushes. Cutters know that saguaros, the signature big cactus of the region, always grow among sheltering shrubs. So a stately old saguaro will not only serve as a signpost for the walkers, but a landmark for the cutters, and the landmark has a scribble of handy bushes around it to hide the wire.

When the truck goes by on the drag, the Oscar sends a message to base. Base radios: "Oscar 21? Oscar 21?" The cutter answers, and he's cleared. If base doesn't clear him at his Oscar, he'll call home. "Base, did you catch an Oscar just now?"

Oscar 25 follows Oscar 21; Oscar 35 follows Oscar 25. If a cutter vanishes between Oscar 25 and Oscar 35, they know something might be wrong. They go to look for him. If an Oscar bleeps and no cutter is nearby, they know somebody done snuck into the country.

Often the drag will have what Kenny Smith calls "hither thither." Hither thither is a scrabble of pebbles and twigs and dirt on the clean face of the drag. It's knocked from the tiny berms that the tire drags raise on either side of the road, and they tell you that someone tried to hop over. You look out beyond hither thither for true sign.

Signcutters know most walkers pass between 11:00 at night and 3:00 the next morning. They can tell how old a track is by its sharpness—even in the desert, dirt holds some humidity, and it is this humidity that defines the track's edges. As a track ages, it dries, and as it dries, its edges soften. Bug-sign is created when small creatures begin to scurry about just before dawn. Often, this hour is the only comfortable moment of the day, and in a burst of breakfast exuberance, lizards, rats, and insects set off in a willy-nilly marathon.

If bug-sign crosses over a walker's footprint, the cutter knows the walker has passed nearer to midnight than to dawn. If, however, the footstep flattens the bug-sign, the cutter knows the walker has recently passed, and is in the immediate area, and is probably in trouble. The sun is up, the temperature is rising, and the day will only get more brutal.

When the cutter sees criss-crossing sign on the drag, he radios another unit. That agent drives to the next drag north and cuts. If he finds sign, he calls the first unit to leapfrog north to the next drag. He cuts it. Sooner or later, the sign runs out, and they have the walkers boxed in between them.

It's when the walkers get far off the drags that all the trouble starts.

Mike F.'s walkers were not only off the drag, they were off the map.

Kenny Smith was working the trailer trash radio, sending more and more units on the Banzai Run. Everybody was heading out there, every truck that could move. They were even thinking of sending out the water-buffaloes, the big water-tank trucks in the fleet. It was a mad scramble as they raced the heat.

From Vidrios Drag, the signcutters started back into the wasteland, cutting, cutting. They started finding corpses. They read the ground and found, after an amazingly long haul, where the journey had all gone so wrong. Some of the illegals had walked over sixty-five miles—a couple of them fell in sight of the freeway.

All you can do, Kenny Smith said, is cut sign, cut sign, cut sign.

The sign tells the story.

The sign never lies.

And the whole investigation became a series of drag-cuts. It started after they had found all the dead—fourteen men; after they had saved the rest—twelve more. The footprints wrote the story. And after the footprints ran out, it was a trail of whispered stories and paper sheets. It was the big die-off, the largest death-event in border history.

Everybody wanted to know what happened, how it happened. The old boys of Wellton were forever changed by it. The media started calling the dead the Yuma 14. National stories focused on the Devil's Highway as a great metaphor for the horrors of the trail. But the agents who saw it all simply refer to it as "what happened." As in: what happened in May, or what happened in the desert. Nothing fancy.

Somebody had to follow the tracks. They told the story. They went down into Mexico, back in time, and ahead into pauper's graves. Before the Yuma 14, there were the smugglers. Before the smugglers, there was the Border Patrol. Before the Border Patrol, there was the border conflict. Before them all was Desolation itself.

| | | | | | | | |

These are the things they carried.

John Doe # 36: red underpants, mesquite beans stuck to his skin.

John Doe # 37: no effects.

John Doe # 38: green socks.

John Doe # 39: a belt buckle with a fighting cock inlaid, one wallet in the right front pocket of his jeans.

John Doe # 40: no effects.

John Doe # 41: fake silver watch, six Mexican coins, one comb, a belt buckle with a spur inlaid, four pills in a foil strip—possibly Advil, or allergy gelcaps.

John Doe # 42: Furor Jeans, "had a colored piece of paper" in pocket.

John Doe # 43: green handkerchief, pocket mirror in right front pocket.

John Doe # 44: Mexican bills in back pocket, a letter in right front pocket, a brown wallet in left front pocket.

John Doe # 45: no record.

John Doe # 46: no record.

John Doe # 47: no effects; one tattoo: "Maria."

John Doe # 48: Converse knockoff basketball shoes.

John Doe # 49: a photo ID of some sort, apparently illegible.

They came to the broken place of the world, and taken all together, they did not have enough items to fill a carry-on bag.

|||||||

Wellton's Officer Friendly, a Latino who looks Italian, bristles at calling them the Yuma 14. "If anything, they're the Wellton 14," he says. "We found them. Yuma didn't do shit." In Tucson, however, they're considered to be the Tucson 14.

The confusion comes easy. The group entered the United States in Tucson sector, and they were headed for a Tucson sector pickup spot. They just happened to have died in the Yuma sector by accident. Walkers are identified by sector, not station, so the Wellton crew was erased from the headlines. Thus Yuma was forever enshrined as the rescuer of the survivors and the collector of the dead.

There were other claims, too. Coming into the game a little late, Mexico declared the Yuma 14 as folk heroes: after all, Mexico loves a martyr, perhaps as much as it dislikes confronting the catastrophic political malfeasance that forced the walkers to flee their homes and bake to death in the western desert. Human rights activists claimed them, too: Our fourteen murdered brothers! Journalists took them as the hottest story (no pun intended) in many years.

Officer Friendly considered all this a steaming pile of Bravo-Sierra.

They were not only Wellton's bodies, he points out, but there were twenty-six of them, not fourteen. "They're the Wellton 26," he says. "All of them are victims, even the live ones. And they're mine."

Nobody wanted them when they were alive, and now look—everybody wants to own them.

|||||||||

Their paperwork got processed through Tucson, as well. The dead were given back to Mexico's care through the auspices of the consul's offices in the borderland. The consul of Calexico flew home with the bodies, their first and last trip by airplane; and Tucson's consul, Carlos Flores Vizcarra, collected the files. The death reports went to the groaning shelves of the Tucson consulate. It was all quite routine, with regular patterns, ruts, and observances.

When a fresh death report comes into the consulate building, the women of the consulate light votive candles. Each desk flickers with a small flame. If you didn't know any better, you would think it was a religious observance.

The reports arrive from the officials, so many that it's getting hard to file them. Shelves are stuffed with them, and piles of reports sometimes accumulate on the tabletops. The Yuma 14's documents, like all of the death reports at the consulate, were tucked into accordion folders, cheap manila packets available in any Target or Kmart. The death packets are known as "archives," and harvest season—May through July—is known as "death season." It is then that lettuce, tomatoes, cucumbers, oranges, strawberries are all ready to be picked. Arkansas chickens are ready to be plucked. Cows are waiting in Iowa and Nebraska to be ground into hamburger, and grills are ready in McDonald's and Burger King and Wendy's and Taco Bell for the ground meat to be cooked. KFC is waiting for its Mexican-plucked, Mexican-slaughtered chickens to be fried by Mexicans. And the western desert is waiting, too—its temperatures soaring, a fryer in its own right.

OTM—Other Than Mexicans—covers all the Central and South Americans swelling the ranks of the walkers. Many Americans don't know that Chinese and Russian refugees cross Desolation as well. And Mexican smugglers are now using freighters to run the North American coastline and drop the walkers into Canada, where the rules are lax and the border— twice the length of the Mexican border—is even more abandoned. Middle Eastern operatives look like Mexicans; as long as they keep their mouths shut, they can pass. Muslim missionaries have moved into southern Mexico, often taking up where Christian evangelists have left off. They set up Koranic schools in Indian villages, and in tribes where the children do not even speak Spanish, they are being taught to read, speak, and write Arabic. Reportedly, the largest al Qaeda training ground in the New World is in Brazil. The Texas and Arizona branches of the Border Patrol have aired suspicions that the smugglers are happy to transport al Qaeda members across the Devil's Highway. In a world of pure capitalism, Osama's crew has the juice: these ultimate OTMs are said to pay fifty thousand dollars apiece.

Of course, the illegals have always been called names other than human—wetback, taco-bender. (A Mexican worker said: "If I am a wetback because I crossed a river to get here, what are you, who crossed an entire ocean?") In politically correct times, "illegal alien" was deemed gauche, so "undocumented worker" came into favor. Now, however, the term preferred by the Arizona press is "undocumented entrant." As if the United States were a militarized beauty pageant.

Maybe it is.

In the strange military poetics of the Border Patrol, the big kill itself is known not only as the Case of the Yuma 14. It is officially called "Operation Broken Promise." Of all the catch phrases of the event, this is perhaps the most accurate.

|||||||||

In the postmortem packets, you will find death certificates, coroner's reports, INS or sheriff's reports, and the pictures. Each report has color photographs of the dead, both in hard copy printouts and digitized on computer disks. The pictures focus on the faces, or what's left of the faces, then the torsos, occasionally the genitalia. Hands are greatly in evidence, but you never see feet.

The dead have open mouths and white teeth. They are stretched in angular poses, caught in last gasps or shouts, their eyes burned an eerie red by the sun. Many of them are naked. Some of them have dirt in their mouths. When the corpses are those of women, their breasts have shrunk and withered and cracked open under the sun. The deads' open mouths reveal gums that have turned to some substance that looks like baked adobe, crumbling and almost orange. They look like roadside attractions, like wax-and-paper torsos in a gas station Dungeon of Terror. For many of them, these are the first portraits for which they have posed.

The Yuma 14 are all male.

Along with dead flesh, the photographs show pants, shoes, underwear. Teeth in close-up. Tattoos, if any. The pants are Latino knockoffs of American designer jeans: Furor, OK Roy, Fase 2000. Most of the underpants are colored, as if the walkers hoped to be stylin' when they got to Phoenix. Blue, red, and black are the favored colors. The underpants are stained, either with urine or other body liquids that have boiled out of the corpses.

Among the paperwork and photographs in each packet is a king-size Ziploc sandwich bag. Each baggie contains the final effects of the walkers, whatever was found on and around the bodies that might be returned to their survivors, or that might be used to identify the dead. Some reports wittily call these men Juan Does. Jane Doe becomes Juana Doe. The women of the consulate open the files and catalog what remains. If you are lucky, they will show you these treasures. As they search for the Yuma 14's archives, they place a fresh folder on the table. It contains a wallet, a few coins, a comb with hair and dandruff in its teeth, and a Catholic scapular. The picture on the scapular is of the Virgin of Guadalupe.

The stench sneaks from the baggie.

The women tell you that they go home with the smell on their skin, in their hair and clothing. Sometimes, when several packets have arrived in their office, they can't wash it off, even hours later. A year after death, files still reek faintly of spoiled flesh. The incense of their death takes over the room.

So the women light candles.

Once their candles are lit, they bend to the task of trying to find the families back in Mexico so they can deliver their grim news. Many dead walkers come from places with no phones, homes with no addresses. The best the consulate can do is call the village phone booth and hope a passerby will answer. Or they track down the mayor of the nearest town, and he then either does or does not find the widows.

In the back office of the consulate, the chemical scent of jasmine, musk, vanilla, fights the smell of corruption. One of the secretaries utters the Mexican phrase for *yuck*. "Guácala." It sounds like something you eat.

The chief of consular security waves her off.

He says, "When forensic evidence fails us, we are forced to register circumstantial evidence."

Forensic evidence would consist of such things as fingerprints. But the nature of desert death is such that forensic evidence is quickly obliterated. The body mummifies. In one of the million ironies of the desert, those who die of thirst become waterproof. Their fingers turn to stiff leather, and the prints are unreadable. On the day the consulate reopens the files of the Yuma 14, they have four bodies undergoing hydration at the coroner's lab. A new corpse, Juan Doe # 78, is cooling in their company. The coroners pump fluids into their reluctant tissue, sometimes for days, to try to plump up the desiccated skin enough to raise a usable print.

The chief's excited. This CSI stuff is fun.

"Your boys," he enthuses, "were only out there three days or so. They're already turning to mummies, but they're not so bad. You ought to see the ones who've been out there a week. Two weeks! Black as leather! And they crack open—red and brown stuff drips out all over the ground!" He pulls a face. "It's a soup. It's disgusting!"

Many of the dead have gold or gold-rimmed or missing teeth, and their photographs offer the final indignity: they have white rubber-clad fingers jammed in their mouths, pulling their lips apart in maniacal grimaces, to reveal these orthodontic details. For these few, it has to be the teeth; there is literally nothing else.

The bodies that are identified are ultimately processed by the Adair Funeral Home in Tucson. They are embalmed, then placed in a cloth-covered wooden casket. This undertaking costs $650. If they are to be flown home, the "air-tray" to hold the casket costs an extra $50. The Mexican consulates pay for the embalming, and other parties—sometimes the governments of the walkers' home states—pay for the flights. For more than 80 percent of the dead, it is the most expensive gift they have ever gotten.

Those who are never identified are registered by the United States. Under their new government-bestowed number, they are interred in the potter's field at the Ft. Lowell cemetery in Tucson. They each get a small marker with metal serial numbers. These Juan Doe burials cost Pima County $760 each.

What of others? What of the phantom walkers from the Wellton 26? Stories float among the survivors that three men walked away. Some call it the Wellton 30. One survivor still maintains there were seventy in the original group.

"They are gone," the Mexican consul in Tucson says. "No, no."

He looks out the window.

"You will never find them."

He rests his hands on the desk and looks at them.

"Perhaps a scrap of clothing."

He sighs.

"In the desert, Levis last longer than meat."

Six coins and four pills, a green handkerchief.

The candles flicker.

|||||||||

Some of the Yuma 14/Wellton 26 spoke Spanish as a second language. It surprises people to learn that many of the "undocumented entrants" are indigenous. Think of the border struggle as an extension of the Indian Wars, the cavalry now chasing new Apaches and Comanches. Much of the human hunting that goes on along the border happens on Cocopah, Papago, Pima, Apache, and Yaqui lands. The Arizona Border Patrol, with millions of acres to inspect, has struck up an uncomfortable relationship with the natives in its path. Tohono O'Odham people, for example, regularly submit complaints of harassment by Tucson sector. A truckload of Indians looks like a truckload of Mexicans to the cavalry.

The Mexican mestizos south of the border, who traditionally lack our nostalgia for the "Indian past," call the walkers "Oaxacas," from the name of the Mexican state that houses one of the largest Indian populations. "Oaxaca" is a code-name for Indian, usually Mixtec. The women are often ridiculed as "the Marias." Some of the Tohono O'Odham call the walkers invading their rez "Oaxacas." The Yuma 14 are still regularly called the Oaxacas.

Indians calling Indians Indians.

The majority of the group came from tropical Veracruz. No terrorists, ex-cons, or drug mules. Mostly, small-plot farmers, coffee growers, a schoolboy and his dad. Some of them were used to seeing up to sixty inches of rain a year—the Devil's Highway would be lucky to get sixty inches in a decade. They walked into the desert carrying soft drinks. Most of them had never seen a desert. Several of them had never ridden on a train, an elevator, or an escalator. Some had never driven a car. Some of them had never even eaten flour tortillas; to them, that was exotic food.

There are two fairly common jokes told about America among "undocumented entrants"—A) Don't drink the water, and B) For good American food, go to Taco Bell.

What we take for granted in the United States as being Mexican, to those from southern Mexico, is almost completely foreign. Rural Mexicans don't have the spare money to drown their food in melted cheese. They don't smother their food in mounds of sour cream. Who would pay for it? They have never seen "nachos." In some regions of the south, they eat soup with bananas; some tribal folks not far from Veracruz eat termite tacos; turkey, when there are turkeys, is not filled with "stuffing"—but with dried pineapples, papaya, pecans. Meat is killed behind the house, or it is bought, dripping and flyblown, off a wooden plank in the village market. They eat cheeks, ears, feet, tails, lips, fried blood, intestines filled with curdled milk. Southerners grew up eating corn tortillas, and they never varied in their diet. You find them eating food the Aztecs once ate. Flour tortillas, burritos, chimichangas—it's foreign food to them, invented on the border.

They were aliens before they ever crossed the line.

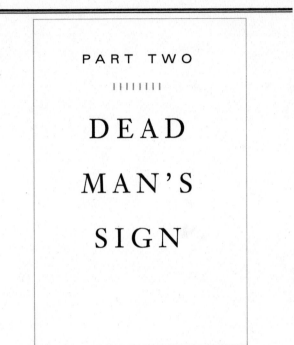

PART TWO

DEAD
MAN'S
SIGN

2

Ⅰ Ⅰ Ⅰ Ⅰ Ⅰ Ⅰ Ⅰ Ⅰ

In Veracruz

The state of Veracruz lies in the southeast of Mexico, its southwestern end anchoring it to the Isthmus of Tehuantepec, the narrowest portion of the country, a slim land bridge that is echoed to the far south by Panama. The steamy waters of the Gulf of Mexico eddy off the beaches of Veracruz, and the air of the tropics is caught here, between the mountains and the sea. The green peaks wear scarves of fog.

Its immediate neighbors to the south are Tabasco and the troubled state of Chiapas. Mexico City lies to the west. Guatemala is less than five hundred miles away. "Veracruz" is a name bequeathed to the region by the Conquest. It means "The True Cross." But its native roots run deeper, and more ancient names still grace the towns and villages of the region: Coscomatepec, Chicontepec, Tlacotepec, Jototepec, Atzalan. Indigenous ghosts haunt the land.

The affix "-tepec" reveals much about the landscape. "Tepec," in Nahuatl, means "hill." Although it is a coastal state, Veracruz is ringed by mountains. To the north, the Sierra Madre Oriental begins; to the west rises the massive volcanic range and plateau that encircles Mexico City; and to the south, which, due to the bend in the geographic elbow of the isthmus is Mexico's west coast, is the Sierra Madre del Sur.

In Veracruz, things weren't going well.

The people were killing themselves working the ranchos on the outskirts. The fishermen couldn't catch enough protein in the sea. The cane cutters couldn't cut enough cane. The small peasant farmers couldn't get good enough prices to cover the costs of planting and harvesting their coffee. Even the marijuana growers were making meager wages once the narcos took their hit off the top and the cops got their *mordidas* (bribes). But it was mostly the collapse of the coffee prices. Locals will tell you that even ten years ago, the surge of illegal immigration to the north hadn't affected them. Rather than going away, they were willing to stick it out, and various waves of semiprosperity affected the region. Coca-Cola and Pepsi hired workers, the fisheries and growing tourist markets took them to the coast, and the region was fertile—crops were variously in favor. In fact, the only illegal immigration that greatly affected Veracruz back then was the unwanted horde of aliens coming north to sample the good life in Mexico: illegals from Guatemala and Salvador were taking all the low-paying jobs in the cities, Panamanians were making tacos and fireworks, Nicaraguans and Colombians were sweeping streets and cleaning toilets. Hondurans in the schools.

Prices kept rising, and all families, mestizos and Indian, Mexican and illegal, Protestant, Catholic, or heathen, were able to afford less and less. Food was harder to come by: forget about telephones, clothes, cars, furniture. Even chicken feed, being *maíz*, was expensive. Pampers, milk, baby formula, shoes, tuition, tools, medicine.

Families continued to grow. The gringos and the missionaries and even the government representatives from Mexico City told them to stop procreating. It was simple: too many mouths caused hunger. But the Pope ordered them to continue being fertile—even condoms were wicked. And in the economy of hunger, which the fat men of the governments did not understand, more mouths meant more chances to survive. With a high rate of infant and childhood mortality, the lower castes, the workers, and the tribal people of the Third World tended to rely on their own procreative gifts for survival. If one out of five died, that still left four to grow up and begin to work. When Madre y Padre became old, ill, infirm, it was only the family that would protect them. No AARP or Medicare in the jungle. Four children, with children of their own, might suddenly represent a small army of twenty, all working, all pitching in, all offering a tithe of food or money or water or tequila. True communism, on a family level.

You'd think that at least there would be beans to eat, but the great Mexican bean-growing industrial farms sold much of their crop to the United States. It was easier for a Sinaloa farm to get the beans to California than to Veracruz—and more lucrative. These beans were poured into folkloric Mexican-looking burlap bags, shipped to Los Angeles, then resold to Mexican distributors. Worn burlap sacks, with their colorful portraits of Mexicans and donkeys and Aztecs, were eventually recycled into useful fabrics in the tropical homes of Veracruz, bean sack curtains for homes that could no longer afford beans.

Between Americanized prices for their frijoles, and the unpredictable spikes in the price of tortillas, the Veracruzanos sometimes didn't even know how they would feed their families. It wasn't just Veracruz. Mexico itself was spending eighty cents from every earned dollar on foreign debt. The vast money machine that was Pemex gasoline and oil bled more pesos than it put into the national economy. The even bigger narco money never made it out of clandestine mansions.

It was a two-way flow. Western Union had facilitated a cash-flood back from Chicago and Los Angeles. Remittance money stormed south from East Harlem and San Francisco, Seattle, and

Skokie. It cost fifteen dollars a pop to transfer funds to the terminals at BanaMex. Western Union became so much a part of the folklore that it had its own nickname, "La Western." People without electricity were well versed in using its computerized services. Bright high school kids from the dirt and thatch villes in the hills could make their way to the city and call up JustinTimberlake.com at the Internet café. If they didn't go north before, they were not going to let the American Millennium pass them by this time around.

Men came home from the United States in cars. Some even had the latest models—new Dodge Ram trucks, bright red, booming Eminem on their CD players. Business-minded fellows could load up at a Texas Goodwill and sell the stuff for twice the price back home. They had their trunks and back seats full of old TVs, radios, clothes, toys. Even guys driving rust-bomb old Datsuns had stuffed them with Care Bears and Walkmen, skateboards and bags of panties. People would spend months' worth of savings on a small used television or Christmas bike, selling for cheaper than the new stuff in the unapproachable Mexican department stores. These fellows offered handshake financing, too: they were, after all, cousins and neighbors and uncles and boyfriends. They kept elaborate accounts in their heads, paid off a few pesos, or a meal, at a time. When the drivers had sold all their wares, they put the old cars on the market, too.

Castoff and donated clothing could be sold in the *segunda*, a rolling flea market set up at each wanderer's house. Some hard workers picked trash at the border's garbage dumps, fixed the castoffs, and resold them at the segundas back home. It was a rural black market.

They built cement block additions to their tumbledown houses, added aluminum to the thatch roofs. New clothes were signs of great success: satellite dishes, air conditioners, boom boxes, guns, cattle, televisions, coffeemakers, PCs, pigs. Some even got telephones. It was unheard of. Villages all over Mexico were suddenly slotting into the Internet, watching CNN.

Families came back with babies who were supposedly American citizens.

The neighbors of these adventure-capitalists watched and wanted. Their children were dying. Dengue fever had made its way up from the Amazon. Malaria was spreading again, and it was worse than before—this new black blood malaria. Corruption, political violence, indigenous revolution in the south. People in Veracruz were looking north, as inevitably as the rains came and the mosquitoes bit.

Enter Don Moi, recruiter for the northern Coyotes.

| | | | | | | |

Don Moi García drove around Veracruz in his big American car, smoking his American cigarettes, patting his Mexican belly that everyone suspected was full of American cheeseburgers. Don Moi was a walking ad for the good life.

Don Moi was trustworthy—the gold watch and the prefix "Don," or Sir, even Sire, took care of that. But he was also a local, living in Tlapacoyan. People knew him—they'd seen him for years, doing his business. He was the godfather of kids, the compadre of their parents, a *tío*, one of the uncles, a neighbor. He was gray-haired. A man, as they said, of substance.

They didn't want to say he was fat, but he had a great solid belly. People could tell the old man was enjoying a comfortable life. That *panza* of his got him plenty of business. Hungry men wanted guts like his.

Uncle Moi.

He drove into the highlands, cutting through jungle and terraced, jewel-bright farmland. He had an exotic cell phone, and he murmured into it, talking to mysterious people in El Norte. He made himself available at restaurants, in cantinas. He could be found wherever men gathered for a cup of coffee with raw cane syrup and goat milk in each cup.

Don Moi was a fixer for the shadowy Coyotes of Sonora, a

Robin Hood figure to the muchachos of Veracruz. A benevolent outlaw with a bushy mustache. And, like all gangsters, he had accumulated a certain place of honor. Many of the poor mothers and fathers who called him "Don" were older than he. Almost nobody called him by his birth name, Moises. Like royalty, he had taken on a title.

In North America, the myth tends west: the cowboys, the Indians, the frontier, the wild lands, the bears and wolves and gold mines and vast ranches were in the west. But in Mexico, a country narrow at bottom and wide at the top, the myth ran north. The Mayas pushed north, and the Aztecs pushed north once they'd formed an empire. Later, the Spaniards pushed north. The wide open spaces lay northward. The cowboys and Indians, the great Pancho Villa outlaws, the frontier, lay north, not west. That's why norteño people are the cowboys of Mexico—not westerners. The Spanish word for "border" is, after all, *frontera*. The frontier.

Along with great adventures in the west, Americans yearned for riches. The Gold Rush and the Land Rush come to mind. For the Mexicans, the Gold Rush lay in those mystical lands up there, above: Orange County, Cicero, Dubuque, Odessa.

| | | | | | | |

More than four thousand men from the region had already left.

New explorers prepared.

They approached Don Moi in small groups. Some of them didn't know each other. He met the Bautistas in Equimite, near their home. The first of the Wellton 26. Heading for a place they'd never heard of, had never imagined. Arizona? The joke was to call it "Narizona," or *the Woman with the Big Nose*.

Don Moi greeted them and invited them to a sit-down. Hmm, hmmm, yes, yes: he listened and nodded. His rings defined arcs of gold in the air as he stirred his coffee. Oh, yes, boys, sure.

Things can be arranged. But they're complicated. You see, it's expensive.

Expensive?

What I do isn't missionary work, boys. It's a business. I'm a professional.

But of course! Claro! Who would suggest otherwise, Don Moi!

My services are the best. So I charge for them.

The ring, the neck chain, the watch. He sipped his coffee. His belly challenged the buttons on his guayabera.

How expensive?

The Bautista boys weren't cheap, but they weren't rich, either. The idea was to go make money, not lose it all before they'd gotten going.

How much is your future worth to you?

Well, chinga'o. We don't have much.

It's sixteen thousand pesos to cross into the U.S. And it's three thousand more for your bus trip and food and lodging to get to the border. Let's say, twenty thousand pesos. Each.

Low whistles.

Twenty thousand pesos! It takes us a year to make twenty thousand pesos.

Don Moi could sense their reservations. But he'd gotten the bite; now he had to set the hook. He beamed at them.

But you won't have to go alone. I'll go with you.

Don Moi, the great father, leading his boys on a field trip.

You will?

We'll go together. Do you think I'd let my clients wander to El Norte alone?

Laughter.

Hook-set.

Of course, you can save some money, if you're men enough to walk in the desert, instead of catching a ride or sneaking into a city.

Man enough! I'm nothing but man, Don Moi! How much will you take off the top if we walk?

I can get you there for thirteen thousand if you walk.

We'll walk.

Don Moi happily started reeling them in.

How will you pay?

We don't know.

Get a loan.

And they did get loans. The going interest rates from local loan sharks for money lent against a plot of land was 15 percent, compounded monthly. They put up their land. A few made deals with Don Moi himself, more than happy to offer them loans against future earnings in the United States. What was seventeen hundred or eighteen hundred dollars when you were going to be rolling in dólares gringos? A few words with his trusted associate, the mighty Chespiro in Hidalgo, and the loan would be approved.

A slight down payment now, Don Moi murmured—whatever they could afford—and a reasonable payment schedule, at a slightly higher percentage rate. After all, Don Moi was taking a great risk in not only delivering them but trusting them to pay him back, and he needed to be rewarded for his trust. A good deal all around, Don Moi would have said.

And of course, they would pay him back . . . Chespiro, well, Chespiro! Don Moi made it clear that he couldn't be responsible for Chespiro's wrath should they shirk their responsibilities to him. They might vanish into the United States, start life anew, be safe forever: who could find them? If the INS didn't find Mexicans, poor old Don Moi couldn't either. But Chespiro. He knew where all the wives and children lived. It was too ugly to discuss, too unpleasant to even consider, so they all agreed that Chespiro should be given no cause to visit the families late in the night.

How soon do we go? They wanted to know.

It takes time. But don't worry, boys. We'll see what we can do.

His cell phone was sitting next to his coffee. They shook hands. His belly touched the edge of the table.

He smiled.

||||||||

Reymundo Barreda was a mestizo, indigenous on his mother's side. Her last name was Maruri, and in the Mexican fashion, he bore her name as well. Barreda Maruri.

He was a mature man, a strong, hard worker with a cowboy's aspect—he favored western wear; his favorite belt buckle, for example, was in the shape of a silver spur. He wore silver rather than gold, either from preference or due to lower cost. His watch was on a faux-silver band. He was a soda bottler by trade when he wasn't tending his land.

He had resolved to go north to expand and reroof his small house as a gift for his wife. A summer of orange picking was all he had in mind. He had already figured out the cost of cement block and aluminum roofing and a couple of bags of cement. Florida. It was warm like Mexico, sunny, pleasant.

His pride and joy was his son, Reymundo Jr. At fifteen, Reymundo was a sturdy student in the regional school system, and he had distinguished himself as a star of the local soccer leagues. Every teen dreams of notoriety or fame, and perhaps Reymundo could develop his soccer skills and play professionally. The thought did cross his mind when he was charging down the field. Full of strength. He had the sheer faith in his father and life that could be expected from a kid whose name meant "King of the World."

In a surprise gesture of loyalty to his father, Reymundo Jr. asked to go along on the trip. He convinced his father by explaining to him that two strong backs could earn more money in a short time than one. And if they both worked like burros all summer, they'd make double the money. They might buy his mother furniture to go in the new room. For them, the planned trip was a gesture of love.

Reymundo Sr. was worried both about his son's well-being. The boy was restless and hungry for adventure. The old man was pretty sure his boy would go off alone if he didn't take him. And he thought of his own lonely journey ahead. When it came time to sit across from Don Moi, he was troubled. But, reluctantly, he signed himself and the boy onto the roster.

| | | | | | | |

Nahum Landa was a dark young man in his twenties with a melodious voice. He had deep black, shaggy hair. Sometimes you had to lean in to hear him speak. His meeting with Moises was oddly Biblical: two men with Old Testament names haggled over details of their exodus. It seemed like a good idea. Nahum was the brother-in-law of Reymundo Sr. If the extended family went together, they could look out for each other.

Nahum was deceptive—his quiet voice, with its melodic quickness, its slightly slurred words, and his sometimes evasive gaze, hid the strong man behind the façade. Nahum was a natural leader. He had no doubt he would survive, no matter what happened to them. And his boys signed up with him, looking to him as a guardian.

| | | | | | | |

There were others signing up.

Enrique Landeros García was thirty years old. His wife, Octavia, was only twenty-three. They had a son named Alexis. He had recently turned seven, and he was ready for school, but Enrique and Octavia didn't have the kind of money school required. Although the Mexican system used uniforms to standardize all classes of students, you had to first have the uniform. Shoes. Supplies. Tuition. Enrique made his way to Don Moi's table for little Alexis—a small illegal venture to pay for a more straightforward chance at a future.

Reyno Bartolo Hernandez was thirty-seven years old. He was one of the older men in the crew. He and his wife, Agustina, had been married for nineteen years. Theirs was a stable household; it could even be called an established home. After their years together, however, they'd decided to adopt a daughter. Reyno went to Don Moi for money to pay for her care. He didn't have many clothes to take, though he did put aside his favorite green pants for the long walk.

Mario Castillo Fernandez was a handsome young man of twenty-five. He was in good condition, a hard worker, his only curse poverty. His wife, Irma, was fiercely dedicated to him. Their love was still strong, though they'd been together since their teens. They had two young children, and like Enrique Landeros, Mario was facing school with no prospects for greater income. And, knowing his love for Irma, there would be more children.

Perhaps he could build a better house. Add a room. Send the children to school in good pants, with new backpacks, known as *mochilas*. Maybe he could buy Irma new furniture. The rumors said he could get to Florida, where it was warm like home. Pick oranges. How bad could that be? He liked oranges. He wasn't afraid to work. He added his name to the list.

||||||||

Don Moi drove from town to town, patient, happy. He called Chespiro, his shadowy boss in Hidalgo.

Yes, yes, it's going well, *jefe*.

I have them lined up.

Several already. Seven, eight.

Don't worry, I'll get more.

| | | | | | | |

3

The Coyote and the Chicken

There are things, unlikely as it seems, that unite the Mexican consular corps and the Border Patrol. In consulates, names of certain Border Patrol officers are spoken with respect, even affection—Ryan Scudder of Tucson is called a gentleman; Mike McGlasson of Yuma is looked on with respect; Ken Smith, at Wellton, is mentioned as a kind of patriarch of the wasteland. The Wellton boys like the Calexico consul and the Yuma consul, and they have a pretty good feeling about the Mexican Beta Group cops, who are the elite agents investigating narco and Coyote crimes on the Mexican side. Aside from that, they seem to see lots of the other Mexicans as communists and thieves.

But the two things that most unify the two sides are each one's deep distrust of its own government, and each side's simmering hatred for the human smugglers, the gangsters who call themselves Coyotes.

| | | | | | | |

The sign is printed in black and blue and red on a white banner.
It faces south.
They have spent good money on it.

> For the Coyotes Your Needs
> Are Only A Business And
> They Don't Care About Your Safety
> Or the Safety of Your Family.
> DON'T PAY THEM OFF WITH YOUR LIVES!!!

The sign has been posted by the Mexican government at
Sasabe, Sonora. It is as absurd a placard as might have been
posted by the U.S. government. Policy wonks in Washington,
D.C., are as ineffectual as policy wonks in México, D.F.

There is no real border here, just a tattered barbed wire fence,
a dusty plain, and some rattling bushes. Walkers face the Brawley
Wash and the Sierrita Mountains coming up from Mexico.

Don Moi never bothered with Sasabe. He wasn't a walker.
For Don Moi, the conspiracy was a thing of buses: the Tres
Estrellas and Transportes Norte del Pacífico bus lines. Then a
quick night tossing and turning in a Sonoita or San Luis or
Douglas motel. A wad of colorful Mexican pesos and a nice
lunch, and back home on the bus. It was all *Playboy*s and
American cigarettes, a tequila and maybe some girls. And so
long, boys! I'm going home!

The border was the problem of others.

|||||||||

The Sasabe sign, which many of the walkers can't read, is the
only thing Mexico is doing to try to stop them from crossing.
The Mexican army patrols the borderlands, sort of, though nobody can find them, probably because the Coyotes pay the soldiers off. Coyote gangs have more money than the Mexico City
sign painters. What do Mexican soldiers care if *alambristas*

(wire-crossers) walk into Arizona? Any one of the soldiers might very well head north himself at some point.

For a while, the Mexican government offered the walkers survival kits with water and snacks, but the uproar from the United States put a stop to that. Americans saw these attempts at lifesaving as a combination invitation to invade and complimentary picnic basket. They were further astonished to learn that Mexico City officials put condoms into the boxes. Of course, Mexico City claimed this was a gesture of deep consideration for the health of all involved. Gringos were deeply alarmed that the illegals were not just coming over to work, but to get laid. They're coming for our daughters! They're coming to make welfare babies! They're coming to party, party, party!

Fifteen hundred walkers a day depart from under the Sasabe sign. The writer Charles Bowden, on a visit to Sasabe in 2003, counted five thousand walkers in one afternoon.

Although our Wellton 26 did not cross at the sign, their trail leads to the region surrounding it. The Lukeville/Organ Pipe border was too busy for them, so they scooted off to the side and tried to backtrack to the Lukeville paths once they were in the United States.

No matter where they entered, they had only to step over a drooping bit of wire fence, or across an invisible line in the dust. Near the legendary crossing at El Saguaro, there is often no fence at all. Along the Devil's Highway near Tinajas Altas, there is nothing but a dry creek bed and a small sign telling walkers: *Y'all better stay out or else we'll be, like, really really bummed!*

Tucson's newspapers described their entry as having been "somewhere between Yuma and Nogales." This is a safe bet—a cursory glance at a map will reveal that most of the state lies between Yuma and Nogales. Several accounts say they crossed at a tiny burg called Los Vidrios, not to be confused with the Vidrios Drag.

A woman named Ofelia, or Orelia (depends on who you ask),

Alvarado runs a small truck stop at Los Vidrios. Many walkers stop at her store before they cross over. Near Mrs. Alvarado's store are signs that warn walkers "USA Prohibido!" Walkers see them, scratch their heads, and continue. At best, the signs imply, in bad Spanish:

TO USE IS PROHIBITED!

To use what? The trail? The sign? The desert? Spanish? Nobody, it seems, told the Yanquis who put the signs up that in Mexico, "USA" is spelled "EEUU."

Mrs. Alvarado never saw the Wellton 26. She told reporters that a young man had gone a few days before they did, and he'd returned, burned black and vomiting blood, after they'd left. He told her God was coming to get him.

So Los Vidrios, as generally reported, was not their crossing point.

Most of the survivors say they crossed at El Papalote. That would be a tiny scatter of wrecks and huts whose name translates as "the kite." The trail probably led them into the Quitobaquito Hills. These confusions and guesses should suggest why it's so difficult to enforce immigration law on the border. Of the men confirmed to have survived from the group, none can agree on where, exactly, they entered the United States. Perhaps only one person knew where they were trying to go once they were here, and that was their Coyote.

From El Papalote, it seems like the myth of the big bad border is just a fairy tale. One step, and presto! You're in the EEUU. Los Estados Unidos. The Yunaites Estaites. There's nothing there. No helicopters, no trucks, no soldiers. There's a tarantula, a creosote bush, a couple of beat saguaros dying of dry rot, some scattered bits of trash, old human and coyote turds in the bushes now mummified into little coal nuggets. Nothing.

The smugglers tell the walkers it's just a day's walk to their pickup point. If they are crossing into Organ Pipe Cactus

National Monument, it's literally a walk in the park. A couple of hours, heading north for Ajo, Arizona. Cold soda pop and a ride to work.

How bad can it be? A day of thirst, some physical struggle— they've lived like that all their lives. The place may be alien to them, but the situation feels like home. After all, they tell themselves, America's a country with a state called Nuevo México. Other states are called Red, Snowy, Mountain, and Flowery; several of them were going to Flowery, and some of the others were going to Northern Caroline to see about making cigarettes. The state of Nuevo México even has a capital city called Holy Faith: Catholicism, New Mexico.

And then there's the hilarious Chi-Cago. ("Piss." And, "I Shit.") It's funny until they feel the cold of winter.

Illegal entry is the sole reason for Sasabe's or El Papalote's or Vidrios's existence. The vans lined up under the spindly cottonwoods have driven from Altar, Sonora, full of walkers. Don Moi was quite familiar with Altar. The bus stopped there, and he often hit the cell phone to check with his bosses: should the walkers hop off in Altar and grab a guide for the Sasabe line, or should they go on to Sonoita, to take part in a more complex conspiracy? Several of our Wellton 26 stopped over in Altar, and it was the merest whim of the head Coyote that put the Yuma 14/Wellton 26 on the bus to Sonoita instead of in a wasted Ford van heading for Organ Pipe. Maybe the Big Man was watching MTV; maybe he was heading for the toilet, or looking for a smoke. He had his phone in one hand, he spoke one word, and on they went to their ordeal.

By the time they were finally rescued, they could have been in Miami.

The ne'er-do-well fence jumpers that galloped into El Paso and San Diego on a quest for chocolate shakes and Michael Jackson cassettes are no more. The New-Jack Coyote is largely the inadvertent product of the Border Patrol's extremely effective interdiction and prevention policies. Good old Operation

Gatekeeper is the mother of invention. San Diego's Border Patrol beefed up the border fence, then placed massive floodlights along it, illuminating the no-man's land between the United States and Mexico. Then, in a burst of creative thinking, it ceased the endless patrolling of the hills and river valleys of the region. Instead, the Border Patrol parked trucks at half-mile checkpoints all along the fence. Each agent is in sight of the next, and all of them are in constant contact as they observe the line. Helicopters still hover, and their versions of the Oscar sensors blip, and night-vision electric eyes scan. The fence in the west extends into the ocean. In the east, it terminates in the wasteland of deserts and mountains.

Unimaginable developments followed. In the region of San Ysidro, the last small town before you get to the Mexican border, at the last U.S. exit off I-5, a big sparkling suburb has sprung up. In this area formerly notorious as a human hunting ground, a dangerous waste of crime and panic, junkies and gunfights, there are now soccer fields and two-story houses that look like they could be in a subdivision of Denver. At the end of all the cul-de-sacs in the development, there is a high wall, and football-stadium floodlights pointing south. Some of the new Latino middle class once crossed that very land in a mad scuttle; now, teens in the neighborhood climb up on their backyard sheds to watch the action in the Tijuana River floodplain.

The hundreds of walkers who once ran this gauntlet are now forced to move east. They rarely try to swim around the western barrier, and if they do, they land in a state park where "fishermen" casting into the surf are often armed feds. The only way to go is out there, back of beyond, away from civilization. And if you go far enough, the fence devolves into a two-foot-high road barrier you can step over. Farther still, and you're in territory much like Sasabe. There are approximately two thousand miles of this kind of terrain to enter.

This new paradigm—walkers crossing Desolation in place of jumping urban fences—has made Altar the largest center of illegal immigration on the entire border. The central park plaza in town is full of Coyotes and walkers. A five-minute visit to the park will garner several offers to cross. Coyotes hawk destinations like crack dealers in the Bronx sell drugs: voices murmur options from a memorized menu, "Los Angeles, Chicago, Florida."

The backs of the Altar vans have plastic milk jugs of water for sale. On the front of each van is a sign made of masking tape, and it says "Sasabe," or "Frontera."

"Carolina Norte. Carolina Sur. Nueva York."

The main grocery store in Sasabe, hardly a supermarket, is winkingly called "Super El Coyote."

The Mexican government's border sign near Sasabe doesn't actually say "Coyotes." It uses the hipper slang of the border. It says, "Los Polleros."

A *pollero* would be a chicken-wrangler. The level of esteem the smugglers hold for their charges is stated plainly. They're simply chickens.

Of course, if you know Spanish, you know that the word for "chicken" is *gallina. "Pollo"* is usually reserved for something else. A *pollo,* as in *arroz con pollo,* has been cooked.

| | | | | | | |

Now, more than ever, walkers need a Coyote.

In the new organized crime hierarchies of human smuggling, the actual Coyotes are middle-management thugs. The old Coyote, the scruffy punk leading a ragtag group of Guatemalans into San Diego via the bogs and industrial parks of Chula Vista, is rapidly becoming extinct. You will still encounter a dope fiend who will walk you into the infrared night-vision RoboCop scrub for fifty bucks, or the homeboy in the Impala who blusters you through the line by being a "Chicano" heading home to the barrio after "hitting the bars," but he's being replaced by the new breed. And woe to that crackhead if the Young Turks get hold of him. He'll be found with his hands tied behind his back and a .9 mm slug in his brainpan.

Even asking questions about these criminals is considered dangerous. Queries into the Coyote operation behind the Yuma 14 catastrophe, for example, elicit three different warnings about being "shot in the head." One gets the feeling that the entire world of Coyotes is waiting, waiting to merge with the *narcotraficante* underworld immortalized by Norteño music and movies such as *Traffic*, waiting to hook more deeply into the white slavery and sex slavery and child-labor rings of the world, waiting for a human-smuggling visionary to unify them.

Gangs are so in control now that walkers who want to go alone, without a pollero to guide them, must pay a fee just to enter the desert.

Criminals are at the gate of Disneyland: they're scalping tickets, and they're scalping each other.

| | | | | | | | |

The criminal operation that lured the Yuma 14 and their companions into the desert and abandoned them was not the biggest, by far. But it was well established, and it operated out of Phoenix, Arizona, and the Mexican state of Hidalgo. It was a family operation. The main man, the Tony Soprano figure, lived in the United States. Or maybe he lived in Hidalgo. He liked to wear cowboy boots, and he kept his figure slim. Or he was never seen by the troops. A voice on the phone.

In Phoenix, it was Luis Cercas.

Luis Cercas, at the time of the Yuma 14 deaths, had contacts in Florida, Illinois, and California. He had a Florida associate, Don Francisco Vásquez, and another roving associate was placed in Mexico. He was the brother of Luis, Daniel Cercas, and he lived in Hidalgo.

Like all of the smugglers, Daniel had an alias, "El Chespiro," derived in part from "Chespirito," the cloying little red cricket of

Mexican kids' TV. (Chespiro! Did some of the walkers think Don Moi was in touch with the television star? Did some of them secretly believe that Chespirito, the red cricket, was a massively powerful gangster? It made a kind of sense to the Mexican mind. Stranger things had happened.) This Chespiro never met the bottom-feeders of the gang face-to-face; he kept in contact via cell phone. All payments went to Chespiro, and all payouts allegedly came from Chespiro.

Chespiro sent people to Sonoita from all over Mexico. A sister-in-law worked in Phoenix, running the administration of the corporation. She organized pickups and human deposits in the double-wides and barrio apartment safe houses. One of these drop-offs is known to have been on Peoria Street in Phoenix.

A step beneath Luis and Chespiro Cercas and their sister-in-law were the soldiers and drivers and guides.

In the Yuma 14 case, the Coyote was a shadowy and notorious figure known as El Negro (with the wonderful Mexican bandido name of Evodio Manilla). He had the universal black mustache. He was short and thin, with an "aquiline" nose and a haircut that in reports sounds like it was a mullet. He wore gold chains around his neck, and he had a curious head-bobbing walk. He had three vehicles, and all of them might have been white. El Negro was also alleged to be the brother-in-law of Luis. *Bada Bing!* It's a family thing.

El Negro apparently worked his way up from an early life as a guide. It was said he never crossed into the United States for any reason once he achieved middle-management status. At the time, he was about twenty-eight.

El Negro, dreaded enforcer and manipulator of Sonoita, Sonora, had a driver known as El Moreno. The Black Man and the Dark Man. Scary. El Moreno affected the black border mustache like his boss, and his round face had a scar slanting down the left side. The combination of the scar and the 'stache made him a really convincing bandido. El Moreno was described as "robust" in the investigation documents.

In Sonoita, El Negro and El Moreno lived together in criminal bliss in a house described as being "around the corner" from an evangelical temple on the west side of town. Local directions are simple: go to the road to San Luis Río Colorado; El Negro's house is there, between the *templo* and a disco called Angelo. Jesus Christ on one side, and party hardy on the other. El Negro sometimes danced at Angelo with his girlfriend, Lorena. Lorena seems to be one of the only people in Sonora not involved with the smuggling gang.

|||||||||

Immune to prosecution, Chespiro oversaw El Negro and El Moreno via long-distance cell phone, and they in turn commanded a small army of soldiers. These were secondary drivers, guards, enforcers, and *guias* ("GEE-yahs"), or guides. Today, these guides are what we used to think of as Coyotes.

They actually cut sign, make trails, and lead the walkers into the desert. Young men, mostly, who are as disposable as the pollos. They can die as easily as the walkers, and the organization will not be hurt. There are always more fools willing.

Smugglers pay locals, like drug lords in the inner city pay off shorties and grandmothers, to cover their operations. Runners. Lookouts. Imagine living in a burning cement brick oven in Sells, Arizona; a guy comes along and offers you two hundred dollars to let him park his van behind your house for two days. Maybe he offers you five hundred dollars to go sleep at your mom's trailer while he waits. You'd be crazy not to take it.

The Cercas crew had a favorite illegal entrant pickup spot in the United States: mile marker 27, on Highway 86, on the O'Odham reservation. Or mile marker 27, or 21, on Highway 85. No one can agree. The Devil's Highway forecasts are always for sun, heat, and impenetrable fog.

But wherever the pickup spot was, when a load of walkers was due, a woman named Teresa would drive up and down the road after dark. Thin, with long black hair, she is our Mata Hari. Teresa must have been bold—even cops don't like to be out there in the dark. The guía would gather his chickens at the mile marker post, and Teresa would then spot them on the drive-by. She'd speed-dial a transport on her cell phone, and one or two vans would depart from their prearranged parking spots.

The walkers, squeezed out of the urban corridors, are relying more and more on the reservation. They cost the Indians millions of dollars a year in cleanup, rescue, enforcement, and land restoration. Hundreds of pounds of garbage accrue yearly: bottles, pants, tampons, paper, toilet paper. Corpses. And the Migra barrels through in their trucks.

This may help to explain some of the frayed relationships between the Border Patrol and the O'Odham people on the rez.

The Cercas gang's western operation centered on Yuma and Wellton, their central operation delivered walkers to the Mohawk rest area on I-8, and the eastern operation—which ultimately killed the Yuma 14—targeted Ajo.

Ajo (Garlic) is a small mining town not far from Why. (Locals quip: "Why not!" And: "Good question!") It's near the reservation. And it's a straight shot to Gila Bend in one direction, and Tucson in another.

The Cercas drivers got Teresa's call and sped onto 86, mindful of Border Patrol vehicles or the unlikely sheriff's cruisers. Cut north on 85, pull up at marker 27, throw open the doors, and hustle 'em in, slam the doors, and be gone. If you were slow or ill, and you missed the van, there you were, waiting for whatever fate would find you.

Recently, a young woman was found dead beside I-8. Someone had dragged her out of the desert and left her like a bag of litter on the shoulder. It is entirely possible that she simply couldn't manage the fast upload into the van and was left to stare at the stars as they drove away. One can imagine the tiresome complications of dealing with a dead or dying woman in Phoenix. The Coyotes are stone-cold pragmatists. Perhaps somebody kicked her out of the van. It was a big freeway—she still had a shot. By desert standards, it was a tender act.

The Cercas's vans would hustle onto I-10 and deliver their loads to Phoenix, where the illegals would squat in safe houses guarded by gang-bangers until they could be shuffled off into wider America. Their United States travel was arranged by big brother Luis, King of the Freeway. All it took was a van, a truck, a car with a big back seat or a roomy trunk. A rear seat on a Trailways bus.

Luis, Daniel, El Negro, and El Moreno plied their trade in the vast reaches of the Cabeza Prieta wilderness. El Negro, El Moreno, and the Dark-Head Desert. It sounds like a Mexican translation of an H. P. Lovecraft story.

||||||||

It will shock no one to learn that Don Moi was said to be yet another relative of the prolific Cercas family.

So this was their system:

The Cercas familia controlled the operation from Phoenix; fixers in other states procured jobs for a fee; Daniel recruited the polleros and the guias for transport of walkers to these jobs, and he oversaw the tides of money, and he made the complex arrangements for housing and transport; Don Moi recruited the walkers—his title was *enganchador*, or the hooker; El Negro enforced and organized the shady doings in Sonora; El Moreno supervised the transport to the launching pad, where the walkers stepped off on a forsaken piece of desert on the brink of El Camino del Diablo, and he sometimes drove.

At the bottom, there was the guía.

4

IIIIIIII

El Guía

Three guides led the Wellton 26 into the desert: one will forever remain anonymous, one is only known by a code name, and one became infamous in the borderland.

Guides are mostly tough boys who earn a hundred dollars a head every time they lead a group across the border. They never reveal their real names, so if they die, they are fated to lie in the potter's fields of Tucson and Yuma. Each one has a code name, so the chickens cannot later identify him. And each one wears bad clothes so he blends in, should the group be apprehended. An army of border trash.

The three guides that walked the Wellton 26 have few things to their credit, but one was the fact that they did not feed their pollos any drugs. Guias now give their walkers cocaine to make them walk faster and longer. Of course, cocaine helps their hearts explode, too. If the guía has been paid in advance, he doesn't care if you get to your toilet scrubbing job or not. It's easier for him, frankly, if you drop and return to dust in the middle of the

Devil's Highway. In 2003, it was reported in the Arizona press that low-rent Coyotes were using a new chemical prod to speed up their walkers. It turns out that ephedra-based diet pills are cheaper, effective, and easily available. The apparent Coyote favorites are over-the-counter "fat burners." A dose of eight pills at a time really gets them hustling.

The leader of the Wellton 26 group was a nineteen-year-old boy from Guadalajara.

If he hadn't inadvertently killed his clients, he would have made about three thousand dollars from the walk, which he'd probably split with his two associates. It was the biggest group he'd guided. Most of them were smaller, parties of twelve or eighteen. Twelve, say, at $100 to $150 a head, five times a month.

He had trained and plied his trade in the Yuma area first, having commuted west from Nogales. He'd worked the drags out of Tinajas Altas Pass, and up around the ABC peaks where the Wellton signcutters patrolled. At some point in the past, he might have been apprehended by Kenny Smith or Officer Friendly or even Mike F., caught, boxed up, and sent back home, only to cross again another night.

‖‖‖‖‖‖

He wore his hair in a silly punk-rock style, cut short all around, with a red-dyed forelock hanging over his eye. He liked to flick it back over his head like an enemy's scalp plopped on his skull. Some survivors said the hair was orange, or blond. To them, anything not black was blond.

They didn't know his name, but they all remembered the 'do. Border Patrol agents still refer to him as "Rooster Boy." A couple of months before the disaster, in one of his other border busts, a federal judge had officially deported Rooster Boy. Sadly for everyone, he came back again.

At the time of the last walk, he lived in a run-down white house in Sonoita with his girlfriend, Celia Lomas Mendez. The house was down at the end of the paved half of Altar Street, #67. He slept with her on a mattress and bedspring resting on the floor of a back room. Cement. Shadowy. The occasional palm tree rustled in the hot desert breeze.

Beyond the end of the paved part of Altar lived his best friend, Rodrigo Maradona, another guía. Rodrigo lived on a dirt and stone alley, but he was close to his pal. El Negro had provided them with cell phones. They're all cybernauts, these polleros, instant-messaging and paging and celling each other like giddy teenyboppers in a shopping mall. They didn't have proper plumbing, but they had da hook-up.

Our boy's Mexican cellular number was 65-13- 85- 21.

His smuggling code name was "Mendez." A romantic gesture in honor of his sweetheart. He still occasionally goes by his middle name, Antonio. Such was his idea of an alias. Antonio Lopez Ramos, aka Mendez.

He had another alias, too. His boyhood nickname among his friends was sometimes Chuy, the diminutive of "Jesús."

This is his true name: Jesus.

Jesus led the walkers gathered by Moses into the desert called Desolation.

Jesus has the inevitable birthday of December 25.

By way of this letter, I ask forgiveness and pardon for what happened in the Arizona desert, because I really am sorry from the bottom of my heart for what happened and it honestly wasn't my intention to lead those people to their deaths. Rather, my intention was to help them cross the border. But we never imagined the tragedy would happen.

But he did. He imagined it. It was no secret, this chance of death.

Every week, walkers are left to die by their guias. It is so common that it must be seen as a standard Coyote practice. A business move.

Wellton agents will tell you any number of heinous stories, as will the Mexican consular corps. Like the group jammed into a van that cut across the Devil's Highway on a mad-dog cross-country run. Once in the United States, the van broke down. The walkers were at least thirty miles from the freeway. The driver told them it was an easy five-mile walk. Then he set the van on fire to keep it out of the hands of the Border Patrol. Said he was going to fetch a fresh van, and he'd be back to pick them up farther along the trail. He, of course, never returned. Many of the walkers died on that stroll. One of them was a pregnant nineteen-year-old woman.

In the summer of 2002, an idiot pollero driver with twenty-three pollos on board went the wrong way on Interstate 8 in California. Lights out. He was trying to avoid a Border Patrol checkpoint. His van crashed head-on into a Ford Explorer and sent it flying off an embankment, killing Larry Baca and nearly killing his fiancée. The hurtling van demolished four cars before finally stopping, twisted beyond description. This kind of smash-up bears a wry acronym among law enforcement wags: DWM (Driving While Mexican).

At least the driver of the van had the good taste to die for his sins. Four of his pollos also died—one of the dead was a Brazilian, and other Brazilians are believed to have been crammed into the van. Some reports list an astonishing thirty-three riders. (This brings to mind the hoary old joke: Q. Why did Santa Ana only take six thousand troops to the Alamo? A. Because he only had one Chevy!)

The guía that time was a twenty-five-year-old former Mexican field worker named Alfredo Alvarez Coronado. He was paid by "an organization" that gave him the cut-rate salary of three hundred dollars per load. Our man Mendez would have scoffed at that minimum-wage paycheck, but Alfredo Alvarez said he earned so little in Mexico—a hundred pesos a day (about ten dollars)—that the pollero work was a windfall. One walk, one month's salary.

Alfredo's walkers had been charged between thirteen hundred and fifteen hundred dollars a head for the hike-and-ride. The drivers in this particular gang were suspected of at least eight other dangerous wrong-way drives on California freeways. Thirty-one of the illegals from the crash ended up in the hospital. It can be fairly assumed that the "organization" that lured them across did not volunteer to pay these hospital bills.

Unfortunate third-class passengers who can't afford a ride on a car seat are locked in the trunk. Some of them are actually strapped to the engine blocks. In the trade, these rides are known as "coffin-loads."

I want you to know that since my childhood my parents have always been of very low economical resources. My parents had to make great efforts just to feed us each day. I was forced to leave school because they didn't have enough economic means to send all four of us children to school. So I decided to leave my family and look for work, and make good money to help my family make ends meet and buy them a house, since they don't own their own home. I worked legitimately at a factory making roof tiles in Nogales, Sonora. The wages were truly very low, and that was my reason for getting involved in the smuggling business.

It didn't take long for El Negro's agents to find Mendez—he was exactly like the walkers he would later lead. Poor, alone, looking for a better life, willing to do what it takes. Like them, he was recruited. Like them, he was welcome to die for the Cercas brothers. There were many more waiting to take his place. There were so many more of him that he didn't even exist.

Mendez and the walkers didn't know they were invisible: on the Devil's Highway, you had to almost die for anybody to notice your face.

|||||||

5

Jesús Walks Among Us

In the sheriff's department videos, the survivors' faces are almost black against the stark white hospital pillows. The camera zooms in close to them. Their features are overwhelmed by the glare. They're nearly invisible in the brutal light.

They wear ridiculous flowered hospital gowns. Many have oxygen hoses plugged into their noses. They are all still weak. Some have IV bottles leaking saline into their veins. A few of them have lips so swollen and cracked that they can barely talk. They hold wadded cloths to their mouths to catch the drool that keeps leaking out. During one interview, a nurse bursts in and says, "We need urine." The man looks down at her and nods, then tries to keep talking as she collects his fluids.

They're in shock. They can't spell their own names. They can't spell the names of the villages and ranches they came from. They look to the deputies, as if the Americans can help them remember the letters. They don't know what day it is. They don't know the name of where they were. When they mention Sonoita, they call it "Sonorita," or Little Sonora.

"Do you know which direction you traveled?" the sheriff asks one man.

He thinks for a moment, then nods.

"Yes. I remember," he says.

He gestures straight ahead with one hand.

"That way," he says.

I I I I I I I I

Do you know who the Coyotes are?

"I don't know who they are."

Are they here in the hospital?

(Looking around.) "Are they here in the hospital?"

Okay. When you crossed from Sonoita, who was leading you?

"I don't know who was leading us."

How much did you pay?

"I didn't pay anything to anybody."

Oh, sure, they brought you for free.

(Looks away.) "Uhhh . . . well . . . you know. It was handled by the legendary Negro. It was probably paid by my brother."

Is he here?

"My brother's here?"

Did he cross with you?

"My brother? I grew up with him."

How do we get in touch with this legendary Negro?

"Oh, fuck."

How old is he?

"How am I supposed to know how old he is?"

How old was the guide?

"Normal. He was a regular age."

What did he look like?

"He had that stupid red punk-rock haircut hanging down in front."

| | | | | | | | |

Jesús had once come from the South, too. He first came north from Guadalajara, looking for work. No one knows if he imagined crossing illegally or not, but whether he crossed over or stayed in the Mexican border region, he would earn more money there than he would at home. He had wanted to buy his mother a house. He had kicked around for a while, never made it into the United States if that was his plan, and somehow ended up in Nogales, Sonora. It's a lively little town just across the line from the somnambulant burg of Nogales, Arizona. Straight down I-19 from Tucson.

Jesús had worked in a brickyard, the San Antonio tileworks in sunburned Colonia Virreyes. He had cursed his fate, looking for a way out. This was no way to live, and it certainly wasn't going to get him a Cadillac or his mama a house. For whatever reason, he hadn't wanted to get into the drug smuggling world. And he had shied away from the teeming world of possibility that was Tijuana. Coming to Nogales in search of success had not been a sign of tactical genius.

In the winter of 2000, he met Rodrigo Maradona, who worked the mud beside him. They hung out socially, became friends. Maradona was a real hustler, moonlighting after his long days in the tileworks at an altogether more interesting job.

In later testimony, as his story shifted, Rooster Boy said Chespiro himself appeared like the devil in the sunny brickyard. Chespiro appeared and whispered temptations in his ear. It's one of the small mysteries of the story. A little more of that border fogbank.

| | | | | | | |

Maradona was eighteen. Thin. He had a badass tattoo of Christ on his chest. Another "chico banda," rockin' dude. No doubt Jesús let Maradona know that he was aching to make some real money. Well, well, well! It just so happened that Maradona was a part-time Coyote! And he was making *great* money. He was earning a hundred dollars U.S. for each pollo he took across the line.

A hundred dollars! Shit, brother, Jesús wasn't making a hundred dollars a week!

A hundred dollars a week! *No seas pendejo, Chuy!* Maradona was making a thousand dollars a week!

The beer sloshed, the smoke rose.

Jesús would sure like to get into some pinche money like that. Maradona told him he could be living large, any time.

It was sounding good. Maradona told him stories—the thrill of outfoxing the goddamned Migra, the excitement of finding yourself alone in the desert with some fine foxy lady, the stuff you could buy. The Coyotes and polleros didn't call each other Coyotes. That was one of the first things Jesús had to do if he didn't want to sound like the Guadalajara hick that he was. He had to get with it. He had to *agarra la onda, buey.* He was ready to get "la onda." Okay, Maradona told him—polleros called each other "gangsters."

Not gang-bangers, who were "pandilleros"; not thieves, who were "rateros"; and not bandits, who were "bajaderos." Honest to God Tony Montana Scarface *gangsters.* Cars, money, molls, gold rings. And they indulged their vices to the hilt. They liked their dope (*mota*), and they liked getting drunk (*andando pedo*) and they loved their dog fights and their cockfights. It was heady. One thing was for sure. No full-time gangster ever had adobe caked under his nails.

Maradona wove the web.

There was only one problem. Nogales was dying. The Migra had the desert sector near town shut down tight. They had been adapting the El Paso formula: big new fences, some kind of human radar, night vision, and more cops. The bastards parked their trucks in a line, each truck in sight of the next, and they just sat there. They watched for hours, drinking sodas, clicking their radios. Everybody in Nogales said they handcuffed *morras* (girls) in the trucks and felt their *chi-chis.* Pinche Migra!

So right now, the action was focusing out west, a mean town below the Yuma border called San Luis Río Colorado.

Orale, it sucked, all right? The dying salty remnant of the Colorado River oozed by, picking up green chemicals and sewage as it went down to the Sea of Cortez. But you could hop a fence right into orange groves in one part of town, and there was Yuma, which was ten thousand times more interesting than Nogales. Los Angeles was in striking distance. It was all happening in San Luis.

Maradona was hooked up with a major operation there. He was heading out soon on a Tres Estrellas bus. All Jesús had to do was say the word, and he could be a Yuma gangster too.

Jesús basically said: What are we waiting for?

| | | | | | | | |

Jesús was of regular size, neither tall, nor overly heavy. He had a rabbit tattooed on his right arm. And then there was that haircut.

His haircut was a classic "rockero" or "banda" style. He probably hadn't seen much MTV, but he had seen the Mexican TV shows that featured pop bands like Maná. Shows like *Control* and *Caliente*. Maybe the gangsters had weenie roasts at the big man's house, and maybe they fired up the satellite dish and watched *TRL* and *Oz* and *Wrestlemania* together.

Most of the stuff on Sonoran radio was crap—Norteño accordion music and lame cumbias filtered up from the tropics. Jesús didn't look like those groups, with their polyester two-tone or even three-tone cowboy suits. He certainly didn't dress like those guys. Jesús looked like El Tri, or Molotov. Jesús looked cool.

And he liked his music, music that was getting bolder and bolder. Even the ranchero stuff was turning outlaw—polkas and ballads sang of the virtues of narcos and Coyotes. The culture had common enemies: oppression, poverty, cops, "the government," the Border Patrol, "La Migra." (Oddly, much border slang made law enforcement feminine: la chota, la placa, la Migra.) Rock songs regularly took the governments of both the United States and Mexico to task, demanding human rights, indigenous rights, political parity, revolution, even ecological responsibility. Like all rock, some songs also enthusiastically advocated smoking pot, getting drunk, and getting laid.

And Jesús and his friends were listening. The banda kids, a terror to the staid fathers of Mexico, were becoming self-educated through a kind of samizdat musical network. Mexican bands, Latin American bands, and even Chicano bands from Los Angeles were throwing down challenges in every genre—pop, rap, techno, metal, el punk. What didn't get on the radio rattled from block-party boom boxes and pirated tapes. Deejays in chi-chi bars played the rude stuff to the delight of partiers and the indifference of the strippers.

Some of the songs were unbelievably bold.

The sly cultural warriors of Tijuana No!, for example, released a rousing rap, "Stolen at Gunpoint":

> *Fuck La Migra,*
> *And the policía!*
> *Fuck John Wayne,*
> *I look up to Pancho Villa!*

The chorus cried:

> *California*
> *Stolen at gunpoint!*
> *Arizona*
> *Stolen at gunpoint!*
> *Texas*
> *Stolen at gunpoint!*
> *Nuevo México*
> *Stolen at gunpoint!*
> *El Alamo*

Stolen at gunpoint!
Aztlán
Stolen at gunpoint!
Puerto Rico
Stolen at gunpoint!
América
Stolen at gunpoint!
We gonna get it back . . .

Aztlán ("The Place of the Reeds") was the traditional home of the Aztecs, a possibly mythical motherland from which the tribe ventured forth on a one-hundred-year walk. It was a land to the north of Mexico City. Chicanos recognize Aztlán as being in the American southwest, and it came to represent the stomping ground of "La Chicanada," or the entirety of the Hispanic west. The Aztecs (Mexica, pronounced "Meshica," hence, "Chicano") walked south, out of the deserts, on their way to what would become Mexico City. They apparently walked across the Devil's Highway on their way home.

We gonna get it back . . .

In this milieu, it was quite attractive to be a Coyote. You could tell yourself you were a kind of civil rights activist, a young Zapata liberator of the poor and the downtrodden. In short, a revolutionary. Coyote-as-Che. Jesús certainly fed himself these ideas, if his testimony is to be believed.

Being a Coyote, even a lowly guía, was also muy macho. Jesús had suddenly gone from being a put-upon poor boy making bricks in the wicked Sonoran heat to being an outlaw. He was Lil' Pancho Villa. He had the immense forces of the United States federal government after him. His own government was putting up signs asking him to stop.

And he had money. He had a crib. He had a good-looking *morra* to play house with. He had dangerous men watching his back. He had a cell phone. He had songs being sung about him on the radio and in the cantinas.

He even had a patron saint of illegals watching over his endeavor.

Toribio Romo was originally a priest from Jalisco. He was shot in one of the many revolts that dot Mexican history. His folk power is ascendant. There are Saint Toribio prayer books that migrants carry with them. There are Saint Toribio T-shirts, religious pictures, and scapulars. And there are tales of Saint Toribio's amazing miracles—heavenly interventions: migrants finding water, migrants escaping certain death, migrants outwitting the Migra, lost migrants being delivered unto the pickup point. Selah.

The famous immigrant's prayer that graces the Saint Toribio's prayer book has even made it into the *New York Times*. It's a kind of United Nations affirmation: "I believe I am a citizen of the world, and of a church without borders." See that? No borders! God said so!

Vamonos, muchachos: next stop, Chi-Cago.

Another prayer: Blessed be the outlaws. Living outside the law was as dizzying as tequila.

Jesús went into the desert a boy, and he was led to believe the rigors of El Negro's world would make him a man.

| | | | | | | |

The forces arrayed against Jesús and Saint Toribio were formidable.

American pundits regularly insist that the border needs to be militarized. In a very real way, much of the Devil's Highway region *is* militarized. The Barry M. Goldwater Air Force Range sprawls between the Gila Mountains to the far west and the Sand Tank Mountains to the east. One of the mountains on the base, ironically enough known as Coyote Peak, is a landmark for smugglers. If you make it to Coyote Peak, you are only miles from I-8 and the turgid waters of the irrigation canals. In the east end of the basin, north of the base, a string of mountains known as the ABCs (Antelope, Baker, Copper) lead you north to salvation. But Marines share the vast base with the jet jockeys, and they prowl the desert in camo Humvees. Air National Guard aircraft fly over from Tucson. Helicopters, jets, bombers. UFOs.

Beside the bombing range lies the Organ Pipe Cactus National Monument. Organ Pipe has the dubious honor of being known as the most dangerous national park in America. Drug and human smugglers use it as a freeway, and officers are at risk every day of their assignments. Law is represented there by armed rangers and the federal Cactus Cops, the officers of the Forest Service, Department of the Interior, and Bureau of Land Management.

Farther to the east of Organ Pipe is the Tohono O'Odham reservation, patrolled by tribal police. South of Yuma, it's the Cocopah Reservation. Between Yuma and Ajo, it's 150 miles of sheriff's territory. East of this area is the Pinal Air Park, a weird landing strip full of bloated cargo jets that shimmer in the heat waves. Local folklore suggests that Pinal is also home to a CIA airbase.

All along the line, the tireless Border Patrol drives, flies, walks. They hit the trails on small ATVs like weekend dune buggy enthusiasts. The heroic BORSTAR rescuers hunt for people in trouble. The secretive BORTAC SWAT troops (called "the hunter-killers" by one Cactus Cop) go on their covert missions. A legendary unit of Customs flits in and out of the night like ghosts, the "Shadow Wolves," Native American trackers who hunt down drug runners. Added to the mix is the DEA, often belittled by local cops: "DEA means Don't Expect Anything." BLM cops. And at each border crossing are the border guards (not, the Border Patrol wants you to know, what they do)—INS agents.

There are also big angry white men in Jeeps, two separate groups of "citizen" border watchers working the western desert outside of Tucson. And the human rights groups are also wandering around, hoping to save dying walkers and placing water jugs on the trails. Then there are the prospectors, drug smugglers, journalists, scientists, FBI, park rangers, Park Service cops,

BLM agents, military police, ranchers, Indians, outlaw biker gangs. Scattered here and there are small groups of militias and "patriot militias," their trailers pulled into secure configurations, upside-down American flags and black MIA/POW flags and the occasional Jolly Roger fluttering in the wind.

With so many hunters trying to catch Jesús, it's a wonder he managed to get lost.

⏐⏐⏐⏐⏐⏐⏐⏐

Jesús and Maradona went to work.

The boys stumbled off the bus in the blighted August sun of San Luis. They made their way to the Hotel Río Colorado, flogged by the brutal heat. Here, they took cheap rooms and waited for word from Chespiro.

Maradona knew the walking route—east of San Luis, where buses stopped at a restaurant near a Mexican army outpost—but Jesús didn't. The restaurant was probably the famous El Saguaro truck stop, traditional jumping-off point for walkers heading north to Wellton, a scene from a B movie, one of the haunted diners full of Mexican vampires and masked wrestlers, the place revealed in the last shot of the film to be an ancient Chichimeca pyramid hidden in a sewage-crusted arroyo. From the front, it's bad walls, white paint, a gas pump, and a soda cooler.

The Border Patrol seems to have a strange affection for its tawdriness. In Wellton Station, there are several framed shots of the joint in the chief's office. Agents take visitors in there and point to the photos of cracked, dirty walls, and say things like "There's Mecca."

People stop here and rest in the heat for a minute, drink a soda, buy a beer, and hike away into the wilderness. The Yuma Desert, the Lechugilla Desert, the Mohawk Mountains, the Devil's Highway all lie ahead. Mexican Route 2 runs at their backs. Beyond it, the black Pinacate. To the north, the bombing range. If they walk for two days, they can be at I-8.

Maradona walked Jesús down the pathways. Then, Chespiro sent the first load of illegals to San Luis. They had orders to find Jesús and Maradona at the Hotel Río Colorado.

Maradona and Jesús had already worked out their contacts with the long-haul Route 2 bus drivers. Now they hustled the illegals to the depot and boarded them onto the bus headed for Sonoita. The driver sold them a "special ticket," since they weren't going all the way—each man could ride his bus for fifty pesos, the money slipped into the driver's pocket. He then drove them east, and when he made his scheduled stop at El Saguaro, he pushed the lot of them off and bade farewell. Maradona and Jesús hopped off the bus too, picked up gallon jugs of water, and together the group stepped into the United States.

At sunset, they shoved off, and the walk went well. It was about thirty miles to Wellton or Tacna. Maradona, the old pro, showed Jesús how to navigate by the mountains. They skirted the Copper Mountains, watched for Sheep Mountain, and followed Coyote Wash part of the way. They walked till dawn the first night, and they settled in to rest during the morning of the second day. It was hotter than anyone expected, and they were drinking too much, but Maradona didn't worry—they'd be in sight of lights by nightfall. And they were. They saw the lights after dark, and they orienteered by the glow of the Mohawk radio towers and the vapor lamps of the Mohawk rest areas. They came up over the railroad tracks and hurried to the spigots of the bathrooms, the cool drinking fountains, the flush toilets. Those few with American coins could buy cold Cokes and Snickers bars at the vending machines. Mohawk rest area was already some kind of county fair for that first group. If they'd been Boy Scouts, Maradona and Jesús would have gotten merit badges.

| | | | | | | | |

They made it their practice to home in on "houses and towers" in the Wellton area. As they trudged toward the freeway, they passed over the irrigation canal carrying Colorado water into the desert. There they might have drunk their fill of fertilizer-polluted green water.

Most walkers die a relatively short distance from salvation. Some walkers fall in the canals and drown. It seems to be one of the cruel tricks of the Desolation spirits, but it makes brutal sense. Most walkers are fresh and strong at the start of the journey. After a day of baking in the sun, they start to get disoriented. They drink too much water. They're dizzy and weak. By the second or third days, when they need their wits and strength about them, they are near death. And they drop, often reported with sad irony in the press, a few miles, or yards, or feet, from water, a home, a road, or a Border Patrol outpost.

This first trip, however, went perfectly. The vans appeared, and the walkers were whisked off to Phoenix.

| | | | | | | | |

But the Border Patrol was catching on to the Cercas gang's routes. After two months, they were getting busted more often, their walks disrupted by the sudden appearances of trucks and spotlights. Those Migra guys made Jesús crazy. The Mexican Migra agents were the worst. Turncoats. Traitors. They hunted down their own people, and they were meaner to the illegals than the gringo Migras were. He did everything he could to avoid their attention. He walked down the loneliest valleys, cut across the darkest washes, and regularly relied on the brush-out.

He dressed like the pollos, of course, in case he was arrested. If he was, he'd be processed and put on a bus and sent back. He learned quickly to keep his head down and stay quiet. The Tucson Migra had this evil trick they'd pull. They wouldn't chase you if you ran, they'd run along beside you, and they'd grab a hunk of your shirt. And you'd be trotting along, wondering, *What is this?* And the pinche Migra would be grinning a little. Then, bam! He'd shove you to one side as you ran, and you'd smash face-first into a saguaro. Any tree or tall boulder would do, but the saguaro trick, that really hurt. Yuma was supposed to be a little different, but he didn't intend to find out. Oh, hell no— Jesús never ran. He shuffled along, acted stupid, which they pretty much believed of him anyway. He accepted water and nodded and grinned and said "Sí, señor" when addressed, as if he respected the Migra.

Of course his name started appearing in Border Patrol reports. But of the thousands of illegals intercepted by the Yuma sector, how many must have come back over and over? Jesús was nothing special. Still, he was becoming visible and El Negro needed an invisible man.

So Jesús and Maradona were sent to Sonoita. Hey, what the hell. It didn't make no nevermind to them: they'd been in San Luis a long time, and they'd used it up. Sonoita was just about as flyblown and Podunk as San Luis, but it was something almost new. And there was plenty of work coming out of Altar. The boys had been doing two loads a week in San Luis. But in Sonoita and Sasabe they could probably up that by another three loads a month. Plus the Migra didn't know them out there—they might get away with it for a year before anybody noticed. Yeah, man, *orale vato, no mames buey*, they were ready. And besides, what were they going to do, tell Chespiro and El Negro no? All they could do was get pumped and pack, head east to the dead heart. Plug in the headphones and listen to Marilyn Manson as the saguaros and volcanoes drifted by.

They only had one real concern. They were going to new desert, to the center of the Devil's Highway. But El Negro had a couple of locals ready to show them the ropes. Nothing to worry about.

Jesús and Maradona boarded the same Mexican Route 2 bus they smuggled walkers on. Perhaps one of their bribed drivers was at the wheel. They paid full fare. No doubt the driver's eyebrows rose. *Orale*, they said. No drop-off today. They got off at El Saguaro for a Coke and a piss, a smoke and some flirting. Then they climbed back on, only starting on their big adventure.

| | | | | | | |

6

In Sonoita

And here they were, getting off a bus again, whiplashed out of air-conditioned comfort into another brutal desert sun storm.

Jesús and Maradona trudged across Sonoita and took rooms in the Hotel San Antonio. Chespiro had paid for them in advance. He kept a whole section of the hotel rented out for his recent arrivals, the Coyote's chicken coop. They settled in and waited for the call, which came soon enough.

A Mexican budget border hotel is not to be confused with a Super 8 or a Ho-Jo's. The rooms are tatty, and the carpets, if they exist, are worn. The beds are cheap and occasionally feature little black periods and semicolons that reveal themselves to be hungry bedbugs. No cable. No room service. The bathroom at the end of the hall is all tiles, and the toilet is often in the corner of the shower, and the whole thing can be swamped out with a dirty mop. Oaxacas and Marias clean the floors. The toilets won't swallow toilet paper, so the bathrooms feature aromatic whitewashed tin buckets full of tainted rosettes. The locks are busted. Home sweet home.

El Negro came for the boys and set them on the path with their teachers, a little fat man known as Santos, and a bad-toothed scrapper known as Lauro. These were not their real names. Later, Jesús claimed he didn't ever know anyone's real names.

The new smuggling route was as treacherous as the old. Yuma sector Border Patrol agents will tell you they patrol the deadliest landscape on earth; Tucson sector Border Patrol agents will tell you they do. It's a peculiarity of Arizona—the worse it is, the prouder they get. Kings of Nowhere, they each want to claim the crown. To El Negro's boys, it was just more damn desert.

Where before, they were expected to maneuver north from San Luis to Wellton, or Tacna, or even Dateland (home of the World-Famous Date Milkshake), this new walk was at least thirty-five, and even sixty-five miles long, depending on whether they were headed for Highway 85 or the big freeway beyond. If they walked straight along the cut trail laid down for them by El Negro's scouts, they could get there in two days, three at the outside. The detours possible to them extended for several million acres.

The few place names they knew were eerie to them. They were in a strange Indian language Jesús didn't recognize. Gu Vo, Schuchali, Hickiwan. It was the Dark Continent.

The land was also rougher here, crumpled and spiked with peaks and mounts. Great wads of landscape reared up all around the path. The Growler Mountains, Mount Ajo, the Bates Mountains, the Granite Mountains, the Puerto Blanco Mountains, Díaz Spire, Twin Peaks, the Sonoyta Mountains, the Cipriano Hills, Growler Canyon, Scarface Mountain, the John the Baptist Mountains, the aptly named Diablo Mountains.

It's a naturalist's dreamscape. For the illegals, it's a litany of doom. The poems on the map read like a dirge. A haunted cowboy ballad:

Chico Shunie Wash,
Tepee Butte,
Locomotive Rock,
Gunsight Wash,
Pozo Redondo,
Copper Canyon,
Black Mountain,
Pinnacle Peak,
Camelback.

That's a busy piece of real estate. If God could take an iron to it and flatten out all the creases, there would be a plain the size of west Texas. And in all that land, there were only a couple of *tinajas*, or natural water tanks, and a very few hidden wells.

Pinacate Lava Flow,
Tordillo Mountain,
Pinta Playa,
Cholla Pass,
Saguaro Gap,
Alamo Wash,
Gunsight Hills,
Burro Gap,
Gu Vo Hills,
Montezuma's Head.

If they cut east and climbed the Diablos, then went up Estes Canyon, they might have found Bull Pasture Spring. Water tanks hide on the south side of the Puerto Blancos, and on the north slope they might have found Red Tanks Well. Going northwest up Growler Canyon, they might have found Daniells Well, or north of that, over old Scarface and below the Lime Hill mine, they might have found Bandeja Well. It's a hard slog, even if you're a veteran signcutter, and you know where the water is. You need a U.S. Geological Survey topographical map. The Coyotes, when they had them, drew maps on notebook paper with Bic pens. Their routes were inferred from freeway maps and road atlases. And none of the Coyotes knew where to find a drink.

⎮⎮⎮⎮⎮⎮⎮⎮

Sonoita was easier to trailblaze than the Devil's Highway. It was a small city, splayed in a northwesterly oblong beside Mexican Route 2 and the Sonoyta Arroyo watercourse. The cemeteries were to the east of town. There was a good paved road to the Lukeville border crossing, and a region between Sonoita and Lukeville was called Hombres Blancos (White Men), which gave newcomers a chuckle. Gringos cut south through town on Route 8, heading to the Gulf of California and Puerto Peñasco, or Rocky Point—Ski-Doo and ocean-fishing wonderland.

For a small place, Sonoita had plenty of cantinas. It had several discos. And it had the requisite border nudie bars.

There were other places of worship, too. Sonoita had been targeted for revival by the great Protestant Evangelical movement battling Catholics to a draw all over the north of Mexico. The war was not merely between Catholics and "Los Hallelujahs." In the Catholic church itself there was a schism between traditional Roman observance and the new Charismatic Catholicism, which borrowed from the Pentecostal traditions and featured shouting and clapping, folk songs and uproar, prophecy and talking in tongues. Alternatives abounded. Mormons and Jehovah's Witnesses, "Los Testigos de Jehová," (known by local wags as "Los Testículos de Jehová") worked the barrios. Karate and kung-fu dojos represented Eastern thought. Northern Mexico has a busy Chinese immigrant community, and it was fully represented by its many faiths, including loyal Taoists. The AA sober club in town introduced a "God as we understood God" twelve-step spirituality. A healthy occult subculture simmered away in the neighborhoods—from traditional and indigenous Curanderas to trance mediums, known as "materias." Black magic cults worked in the deserts, and Santería cells worked their mojo. Koranic missionaries were the latest wave to penetrate Mexico. The Imams were making their way north, on their way from teaching the Indian kids in Chiapas and Veracruz how to speak and read Arabic. The Baptist missionaries in their little barrio Bible studies knew what they were speaking about when they preached that "Powers and Principalities" battled in the air over every sinner's head.

Like many border towns, Sonoita offered people better pay than what they could scrape together in the interior; not all locals had plans to cross the border illegally. The San Antonio Hotel was only one of the inns that set aside rooms for "Oaxacas." The rooms were often crammed with ten or twelve nervous people and the bill was paid whether there was toilet paper or not. Sheets? Who was going to complain about sheets? The tenants were sometimes in the rooms for only a few hours, then they were gone. At most, they'd be there a day and a night; rarely did they last more than two. The hoteliers could have simply kept plain rooms, empty except for a slop bucket in a corner, and they could have gotten full price. Some of them did.

Jesús and Maradona, camped out in their rooms between training runs, smoked and watched TV and read comic books. They went out at night and drank. During the brutal daylight hours, they squatted and sweated out their hangovers in front of fans. In this middle period, Jesús met his beloved, Celia Mendez. Nobody knows if she worked at the hotel, or was visiting for some reason. Later reports list her as "Mrs. Mendez." Maybe she was escaping a failed marriage.

In love, Jesús left his hotel digs and moved into Celia's house on Altar. Maradona followed soon after, renting a room down at the dirt end of the street. The runs must have already begun since Maradona could afford rent. And Jesús, now adopting his beloved's last name as an alias, became Mendez. Mendez and Maradona—it had a nice ring to it.

El Negro had the whole thing worked out, a science. The walkers came in by bus, pulling up the long Route 2 from deep in the interior. Mendez, Maradona, Santos, or Lauro met them at their hotels. They either stayed at the San Antonio, or the appropriately named El Sol del Desierto—the Desert Sun.

A night or so before the run, they were whisked across the street from the San Antonio to a ramshackle rooming house known as La Casa de los Huespedes. It was supposed to be a two-story building, but the owners had never gotten around to finishing the top floor, which had become an open tarpaper space handy for hanging laundry. It also lent itself to service as a lookout post. This safe house was the province of El Negro. Although he reserved it for them, his clients paid for the privilege of sleeping there. The manager, Nelly Muñoz, charged them each fifty pesos per day. The groups were always between fifteen and twenty people in size. These loads came through three times in a good week—easy money for Nelly.

The short hotel stay was apparently the last hoop the walkers had to jump through. It was a favorite nightmare of the Coyotes that the Migra's black-clad BORTAC monsters would come out of the sky on ropes, infrared goggles glowing horribly in the night. Sometimes El Negro, in an absurd bit of spy-game paranoia, would appear suddenly and quietly order the walkers to rush to Nelly's and hide, there to await further orders. Then he would hurry off in his pickup, casting glances all around lest he be found out. As if anybody in Sonoita cared.

|||||||||

The Saturday before the fatal walk began, Mendez and Maradona had taken a group across the Devil's Highway. It was a long, arduous walk, but it was uneventful. They crossed the Quitobaquito Hills, heading north, then they cut west and approached Ajo. They stuck to high ground, baffling the Migra's drag system. By walking high, they could only be spotted by cutters scanning with optics, or by Migra overflights. The planes were easy enough to evade. This ground was so rough and crooked that all you had to do was squat under a paloverde or a mesquite, or hug a creosote. Mexican skin, from the air, is hard to tell apart from the ground. Knowing this, pilots often just fly in circles looking for telltale points of white. Bones. The bones come right out of hiding, as if the dead feel there is nothing left to lose.

The walkers made it over Bluebird Pass, and they could see Ajo as a small cluster of lights in the unmitigated dark velvet of 1:00 A.M. It always seemed like madness to the clients that the guides were pressing past Ajo—they could see roads and gas stations and stoplights, they could practically smell the hot dogs and beer. But the guias knew better. Ajo was just a sign they were cutting.

They got past town, and hours later they arrived at a water tank beside a paved roadway. This nameless outpost was the El Negro gang's chosen rendezvous. There, the group rested and drank as they waited for the pickup. But instead of their own driver appearing, a Border Patrol truck found them. Maradona managed to escape with one pollo, running into the scrub. The two men went on to Phoenix. Mendez and his group of twelve were apprehended.

One of the Border Patrol guys saw that Mendez had a rabbit tattoo on his arm.

"What's that supposed to mean?" he asked.

"What?"

"The rabbit."

"The tattoo?"

"Yes, the tattoo. What does the rabbit tattoo signify?"

"Nothing."

"Gang sign?"

"No."

"Is it some kind of Coyote code?"

"It's a rabbit. I like rabbits."

If the Migra had realized who they had in the holding pen, the Yuma 14 might be alive today. But somehow, Mendez wasn't recognized. They were looking for Jesús Lopez Ramos from San Luis, not some Rabbit Mendez of Sonoita.

Another disturbing element of this bust was the water tank itself. Once it had been discovered by the Border Patrol, it was compromised. Forever after, the lifesaving water stop would represent a game of roulette.

Among these arrested walkers were three brothers from the state of Guerrero. Mario González Manzano, Efraín González Manzano and Isidro González Manzano were from a small village near Chilpancingo called Villagrande. Their family home did not have telephone service. They had gone to the Coyote's men in Guerrero, south of Mexico City, and sought passage to the north. There wasn't enough money in the family to take care of one brother, much less all three, and the elders, and the young ones.

The Coyotes put them on a bus for Tijuana, where they were going to cross into San Diego. They were repeatedly foiled by Operation Gatekeeper. Pinche Migra! An associate had called Chespiro Cercas on the cell phone and made a case for them. They were good boys, hard workers. They deserved another shot at the border. Just to prove they were good boys, they'd all taken menial jobs in Baja California. They weren't wasting a minute without earning something.

Brothers were good, a working unit that the Cercas gang could control. Each brother could be threatened or hurt if need be. But if they worked well together, they'd be earning big. If they got into a yearly trip, they'd owe Chespiro money forever.

Chespiro ordered that they be shipped to San Luis, and then—after that didn't work out—they mounted the famous bus to Sonoita and tried again.

Bus after bus after bus: they must have thought el Norte was nothing but bus lines.

The brothers had been living in crap motel rooms for weeks,

and now they'd been caught. They were angry. Enough was enough—they demanded yet another shot at it, and soon. El Negro, in an uncharacteristic spasm of humanitarianism, offered them the next walk—May 19—for their trouble.

"Orale," the brothers said.

They shook hands.

| | | | | | | | |

Back at the safe house, Nelly's rooms were getting full. El Negro was looking to sign up thirty walkers for the trip. Thirty was some sort of magic limit to the Coyotes—few groups ever grew to that limit. There were practical reasons for this. Large groups were harder to control, and they were very hard to hide. The González brothers nodded and muttered hello and crammed themselves into the already stifling rooms of Nelly's house of ghosts.

| | | | | | | | |

Down in Veracruz, Don Moi and his boys were on their way.

The walkers had left their towns in pickup trucks, or small regional buses.

They gathered at the bus terminal and boarded the bus Don Moi had rented for them. A charter. They felt like millionaires.

El Norte. It was a trip of over two thousand miles. The bus was long and fairly modern, a long-haul cruise liner with two toilets in the back, tandem drivers who traded off sleep shifts as they drove. These highway behemoths were known as *"doce ruedas"* because they were powered by twelve-wheel drives. The bodies of the big cruisers were split-level, with a set of steps behind the driver leading into the interior, a tinted sunroof above the seats. Behind the driver, there was a bench seat, where chatty passengers could sit sideways and talk as they stared out the vast front windshield. Reymundo Jr. spent time there, watching the landscape roll by.

Poor people carried their own food on buses. Families boarded the bus with white paper packages of tortillas, small pots of beans, slabs of yellow cheese, candied yams and cactus—*camotes* and *bisnagas*. They made tortas of bolillo rolls and ham and chiles. These meals were often better than the food available in the roadside taco stands and in the dusty bus terminals along the way. Several of the Moi crew carried lunch bundles.

Their few possessions were tucked overhead in the racks above their seats. They toyed with the reading lights and the recliner buttons. The toilets in the back were some of the first flushers some of them had used. Laughter. Some small prayers, muttered in discreet whispers, the sign of the cross ending in kissed crossed fingers. *Journey mercies. Let us arrive safely. We need to get to the border. Help us get into the desert. Make us strong.* It was more comfortable than the chairs in their homes, but the air conditioning was too cold.

| | | | | | | | |

All roads lead to Tenochtitlán. Mexico City is the hub. The big roads converge here and disperse in all directions.

The boys gawked as they approached the great city. Few of them had ever seen anything like this. The occult volcano, El Popo, rose in snowy splendor as the bus came down through pine-covered slopes that could have been in Colorado. The filthy high tide of pollution met the road in the mountains, and the orange mist moved among dying trees like fog. As they dropped into the overpopulated valley, El Popo was gradually erased from sight. The sky turned gold, and the light that hit the streets was brown. Endless grids of buildings spilled into the distance. Thousands of old green VWs, Mexico City's taxis, jostled for position. Traffic jammed tight at intersections. They watched for the fabled UFOs of the city—los OVNIS—but it was too hazy to see the sky. They saw a great white roller coaster, known in Spanish as a Russian Mountain, beside the highway.

And into the bus terminal and the wait for the drive north. A cigarette. A Coke. A candy bar. A quick piss in the stinking troughs in the big rest rooms.

Buses headed north can catch Highway 57, through San Luis Potosí, or 15, that cuts across country to Guadalajara. Sooner or later, they get on 45, and this heads northwest to Ciudad Juárez. In the old days, before the Migra closed it down, El Paso/Juárez was a target destination. Now, they had to move west.

| | | | | | | | |

They saw many wonders as they traveled north. In some of their ancient beliefs, north was the direction of death. North was the home of winter, and the underworld could be found there. They went from jungle to rain forest to pine forest, from pines to plains, and from plains to desert and volcanos.

They gawked at the worms of snow on the highest peaks. They stared at the pine trees, the roadside deer. The big cities were no more amazing than the dry lands they entered, the maguey and burros of the heartland, the cacti and plains of the north. The ones who knew geography told the others where they were—the states with the strange names: Zacatecas, Chihuahua. They passed through a hundred towns, a scattering of cities. They crossed little rivers, watched a thousand beaten cafés and gas stations whip by, burned out hulks of ancient car wrecks, white crosses erected along the highway where their ancestral travelers had perished. The whole way was a ghost road, haunted by tattered spirits left on the thirsty ground: drivers thrown out windows, revolutionaries hung from cottonwoods or shot before walls, murdered women tossed in the scrub. Into the Sierra Madre Occidental, the opposite side of their continent.

It was a dream of speed for men who had not sped before. An avalanche of details and bafflements: army patrols in green trucks, dead donkeys bloated to the point of exploding beside the road, armadillos, empty broken white buildings, crippled children writhing in their chairs and taking the afternoon sun in small dust-smoked town squares. Walls whitewashed and painted blue, red, peach, green. A black freight train struggling toward Durango, seemingly covered in old oil, heavy as a mountain as it scraped down the rails.

Mexican towns full of Mexicans, so like them, yet so different from Veracruz.

Aguascalientes, but they saw no "hot water" anywhere. Victor Rosales, but who was he? Why did they name a town after him? Fresnillo, or the Little Ash Tree, whipped by, but they saw no fresnos beside the road. Or were they those distant trees?

Oye, buey, es ese un fresno?

Quién sabe.

Allí, cabrón. Ese árbol.

Cómo chingas, buey. No jodes.

No mames.

Ya pues, pendejo! No me vengas con pendejadas.

Fresnillos. Bésame el culillo.

Nahum looked out the window, silent. His seat companions shook their heads and went back to sleep. Don Moi didn't like all the hilarity—he preferred to remain invisible. He never knew when the Mexican immigration police were cooperating with the gringos. He dreaded Federales and dark cells where the boot and the electric wire hooked to the testicles were the rule. Better to keep quiet and get the job done. High spirits were a bad precedent. This wasn't a vacation.

They slept sitting up. Brothers leaned against brothers. The boy slept tucked against his father, his gray comic books in his lap. Loners leaned against the windows, pulled their billed caps over their eyes, and tried to nap, keeping their shoulder away from their snoring neighbors. The nude women in the crumpled magazine splayed themselves and made promises no one could keep. In the *Alarma!* crime tabloid, pictures of dead illegals didn't even make the front cover, unless they'd been dismembered by a train. They were inside, among the suicides and the human fingers found in bottles of salsa in border diners. They were so passé they didn't even merit color.

Cuencamé, Pedriceña, Dinamita—a town named after dynamite.

There was nothing delicious in Delicias. Nombre de Dios, the Name of God, lay in the terrible outland.

New languages began to assert themselves. Nahuatl was far behind them now. Strange Chichimeca names floated by: Meoqui, Julimes, Coyame.

They saw a sign for a place called Cuchillo Parado, the Erect Knife. There was laughter over that in the bus.

Nudge-nudge, is your knife erect?

That's not a knife, brother, that's a machete.

You may have a machete, my friend, but in my family we have Samurai swords!

That thing? Where I come from, that's a toothpick.

Ciudad Juárez, large in Mexican myth, second only to Tijuana in their minds, the wetback's promised land, was a sprawl of towers and dust, desert, and trains: nothing there, not a tree, it looked like, not a drop of water. The Rio Grande, known to them as El Río Bravo. Don Moi pointed out El Paso, Texas. Some dark peaks, more warehouses.

Where?

Across the river.

That's a river?

They couldn't see the Río Grande. They could see Mexican freight trains. Black mountains. And they could see the endlessly rushing traffic of I-10 on the American side. They didn't know that this same freeway, far in the west, would be their ultimate destination.

| | | | | | | |

Weary, sleepy, some of them feeling sick from the bad food and the constant jiggling, they headed west. They were driving parallel to the Devil's Highway, at times only yards from the U.S. border. It just looked like more Mexico.

Agua Prieta, Cananea, Altar—where Don Moi made his call to Chespiro and was told to bring 'em on in to Sonoita—Caborca.

Finally, they arrived in Sonoita. Heat and horns, street dogs and northern odors. Another sad dust-dry desert town. They were hustled off the bus and rushed to the motel. They fell about the dark rooms and slept fitfully. In the morning, the legendary Negro roused them and sent them scurrying to Nelly's safe house. To wait. Be ready, they were told—we'll come for you and you'll have to jump. Nobody knew how long the preparations would take.

Fifty pesos here. Fifty pesos there. They were just bleeding money.

Don Moi didn't make it to Nelly's. By the time they wondered where he was, he was on the bus, heading home.

7

A Pepsi for the Apocalypse

SATURDAY, MAY 19.

It is easy to imagine Mendez's morning. Oh, shit, the alarm clock's going off too early. Six o'clock. Last night was Friday, party night. Dancing with Celia. Drinks. Cigarettes and laughter, up too late with the gang. Too late, too tipsy to make love.

Saturday mornings suck.

Headache.

Mouth tastes foul.

Celia is still in bed, her hair scattered over the pillow.

On the radio, El Gran Silencio, singing "Los Chuntaros del Barrio."

A small lizard scuttles across the wall, one of the little desert geckos. Mendez scratches himself and gets up, puts on his ugly walking clothes, brushes his teeth, careful not to swallow the tainted city water. Pees in the low toilet, its water barely there from lack of pressure, the tin can in the corner full of wadded toilet paper. Digs around in Celia's fridge for something to eat, stirs some instant coffee into boiling water. He's always careful to boil it fully so he won't get sick. Otherwise, it's bottled water only, and that gets too expensive. And where's that pinche Maradona? It's seven, that lazy bastard. A tortilla heated on the blue flame of the stove, a smear of frijoles and salt.

Water and gas come in old trucks that regularly clank down his street. The gas for the house comes from a whitewashed or silver tank sitting on a small cement pad out back. Several of the neighbors still have outhouses and use buckets and washbasins. It's a noisy barrio—when the mailman comes, he blows a loud whistle to let them know he's there. Traffic cops blow whistles. So do kids. Everybody's blowing a pinche whistle.

Sellers hawk their wares as ice cream carts jangle by with their little bells and the newspaper man hollers and the corn-cob man trundles along shouting and the weirder salesmen of obscure items parade through: goat-cheek tacos, broiled tripe, and *tejuino*—fermented maize Indian brew. Old-timers say tejuino is fermented by taking a chunk of human shit and wrapping it in a cloth and letting it fester in the mashed corn.

Dogs bark. Old buses gulp and grind through the gears. Beat pickups with loose tailpipes roar. Kids yell. Even roosters crow down among the tattered banana trees of that blue-and-white house where the blacktop ends. Pop! Pop! Pop! Some *pendejo* is already setting off firecrackers. Either that, or some drunk is shooting his wife.

The street is already hot. Man, it was eighty-nine degrees all night. Mendez feels bad—he's already sweaty. He takes his morning crap, trying to get his bowels empty so he doesn't have to worry about it on the trail—hard to keep the pollos in line when they've seen you squat in a bush. He opens the window and sits and looks out at the deceptive green of the back yards of Sonoita. Calculates his profits. Perhaps, for a moment, he dreams of far Guadalajara, and his mother hoping he will someday build her a home.

He's not scared, not anymore. But he's always apprehensive.

And it's a pain in the ass, this hiking in the desert. You'd be stupid not to worry about the walk.

Bids farewell to his woman.

Steps outside, works his baseball cap down over his rockero forelock, slips on his shades.

Sonoita smells like bad fruit and sewage. Blue clouds of exhaust leak from the dying cars. He walks down to Maradona's and pounds on the door. No answer. What the hell? He calls out a few friendly insults—Oye, huevón! Pinche buey! Orale, pendejo! Levántate, cabrón.

But Maradona's apparently gone. Either that, or he's so drunk Mendez can't wake him. *Damn! Door's locked. Windows too dark and grimy to see through.*

Mendez will always wonder what happened to his homeboy. Having started his pollero career in Nogales, Maradona has regularly walked the pathways to the east and west of Tucson. He's the one who really knows the Ajo route. Mendez hits the celly and tells El Negro that Maradona, that *puto*, isn't in. El Negro can't be happy about that. Woe to Maradona when El Negro has a chat with him.

All right, El Negro says. I'll handle it. I'll call Santos and Lauro.

Oh, no, not those losers.

It says a lot about Maradona that he has to be replaced by two other polleros.

Mendez was going to get a ride from Maradona, too. *Chingado!* He grabs a blue-and-white barrio bus and heads downtown.

||||||||

The walkers were stirring at Nelly's. Most of them didn't know each other. The small family groups stuck together. They ate what breakfast Nelly had thrown together for their fifty pesos. Most of them were used to lighter fare than what the norteños ate; an egg or two, a corn tortilla, some fruit. You could always knock down a mango or a papaya, but you couldn't always afford fried beans. Half of them were dead men, they just didn't know it yet.

Unexpectedly, Mendez and his henchmen appeared. The guys from Guerrero knew Mendez from the failed trip last week. They didn't know these other two Coyotes, Santos and Lauro. Santos was fat, hardly a fit hiker. And Lauro was skinny, with curly hair and bad front teeth. He had the requisite bandido 'stache. The other two gangsters were clean-shaven. The Guerrero boys nodded to Mendez.

"Hey," he said, "get over to the store and buy water. You'll need water for the trip."

"How much?" one asked.

"Enough," he said. To another, he said, "A bottle."

They hustled out into the sun.

"Meet me at the bus station," he said. "Be there by eleven."

The gangsters went one way, and the pollos the other. They went around the corner, to the small store. They bought candies and chocolates and wicked salted prunes called "saladitos" and sweetened chile paste in stained plastic envelopes. They bought small water bottles and jugs. A few of them had cold Pepsis for breakfast, and they put bottles of Pepsi in the bags, thinking a nice cool soda would be just the ticket once they got into the desert.

They moiled around. In small groups they wandered to "La Central," the bus station, lines of travelers converging in noisy tumult. Children scattered, mothers scolded. Old men stood on crutches. A small girl could not hold her water any longer and peed on the floor, between her mother's great bundles of clothing. The walkers stuck together, nervous and lost in this strange place. Outside, buses rumbled in their berths, destinations tattooed on their brows: TIJUANA, MAZATLAN, CIUDAD JUAREZ, MEX D.F. Voices blasted over the buzzing speaker system.

"Attention, please. Gate five. Gate five."

It was 11:45.

"Gómez-Palacio and points south. Now boarding at gate five."

Mendez appeared and told them to get it together. Don't look ragtag, man, don't look lost. Look NORMAL, cabrones. Don't draw attention. Get in a line! Lines don't catch anyone's eye. Look like you're going somewhere, boys!

He put them against a wall and told them to wait there.

He had his baseball cap off. The walkers didn't know what to make of the Mendez forelock. It hung down to the bottom of his nose, and he delighted in whipping it back over his head.

It made him look like a *pendejo*.

Oh, well. They didn't have to love the guy. They just had to follow him.

Mendez rushed outside and made his way down the line of buses. He stepped into a Pacifico bus and had words with the driver. Mendez and the driver shook on their deal, and he collected the boys and told them to hustle. Fifty pesos each. Everything in Sonora cost fifty pesos! Some of them thought he was going to handle the fares—they'd paid enough—but, like the cost of Nelly's rooms, it was their problem and not his own. They dug into their meager funds and paid the driver.

The bus driver pocketed the money and didn't say a word. He closed the door and backed out. The group watched through the dusty bus windows as the shadowy travelers in the station watched them back. The bus sighed into the sun, then hove down the driveway and into the streets. The boys were sightseeing, thinking, *Adios, México!* Many daydreams about the United States, daydreams about the walk ahead. Jokes. Daring boasts.

The walkers had bags, or small backpacks, and an average of eight liters of water each.

The driver took them down the highway at top speed. Mendez told them to say nothing when they got to the checkpoint. Soldiers stopped the buses and inspected them for . . . what. They didn't know. Drugs? Whatever. "Look like you're going someplace," Mendez said. He told one of the guys to tell them he was on his way to San Luis, which was a smart suggestion, since they were going in the direction of San Luis.

The soldiers boarded the bus and snooped around, then waved them on. They never said a word to the walkers.

The driver only went a few kilometers beyond the post, to the little patch of dirt known as El Papalote.

Mendez said, "Pull over here."

"Here?" said the driver.

"Right here. Drop us off at this sandy spot."

"Want me to take you up to the rest area?"

"No. This will do. Drop us off right here."

"Whatever you say," the driver replied. It wasn't his business if these guys wanted to hop off a cool bus in the middle of nowhere.

It was now about 1:30.

The walkers stumbled off the bus. Some of them were already hitting the Pepsis.

"Get your things and let's go," Mendez said.

They got all their bags together and choked as the bus pulled away, washing them in fumes and dust. They waved their hands before their faces and waited for a truck to scream by going the other way. The driver knew what they were doing. The United States was less than one hundred yards away. He raised one hand and was gone.

They trotted along the road, Mendez in the lead, the other two gangsters taking up the rear. Nobody told the walkers anything. They thought they were going to jump a big fence and hide in trees as helicopters bore down. But they ran in sand, slipping and struggling, and they dropped into a dry wash and up the three-foot bank on the north side, and they stepped over a dropped and rusted barbed wire fence.

"Los estados unidos, muchachos."

That's it? That's the border? This is North America? It don't look like much!

Their first walk in the United States lasted for five minutes.

||||||||

They reached a hill, and Mendez said, "I have to go get the ride."

Nobody ever knew why they had to take a ride. They thought they had just taken the ride. Why couldn't they just start walking? It was never explained.

But he told them to wait, so they waited. Mendez walked down the dirt road and disappeared around a bend.

One of the Guerrero boys asked Santos, "How long do we walk?"

"We'll walk all night tonight," he told them. "Be there in the morning."

Lauro was telling another, "We'll walk two days, probably. You'll get there in two days."

"We'll start walking about four," Santos said.

"We get going around five, maybe six," Lauro said.

Both of them said it was important to get started when the heat was starting to abate.

Santos announced: "Here comes the van."

A primer-gray Dodge Ram van appeared. Later, survivors would say it was a Ford Bronco. Some of them would also insist that seventy men got in it. Magic realism.

Mendez jammed them in and El Moreno drove them around in the desert. It was a seriously uncomfortable ride. The van banged off-road shortly after leaving El Papalote. The men, sitting on each other, knocking heads, cracking chins off shoulders, were tossed around like laundry. Though the drive was reliably reported to have taken ninety minutes, their level of discomfort is indicated by their testimony that they drove for two, three, and four hours.

El Moreno did his surreptitious routine, sliding around lots of dust trails, ducking phantom helicopters under acacias and paloverdes, busting onto the Devil's Highway and speeding back toward Sonoita. Finally, they arrived at a "big rock." No shortage of big rocks, but they had apparently found the big rock that signaled the entry to the path to Ajo.

The van disgorged the walkers and sped back toward Mexico. They stood around for a moment as Mendez briefed them: they'd walk at night, just a couple hours, three hours max . . . maybe eight. And if for some reason they were surprised by morning, they'd settle in the creosote bushes to wait out the sun. Each of them was responsible for his own water. They held up their jugs like kids at show-and-tell. Mendez was the expert, after all. He repeated it was just a matter of hours to the pickup spot, something he would repeat like a litany during the entire walk. They'd be there by the second night for sure. Everything was under control. They were a little early, that's all. But he was impatient and still a little irritated with Maradona. It was just one of those days. So, *qué la chingada*, let's start now—we'll get there quicker.

The tradition was to arrive at the big rock at three, then walk into the night. But they'd beat the clock. An extra hour or two of walking in triple-digit heat, guzzling water. Getting sick before sunset, but not knowing it.

Orale, Mendez told them. Let's do it.

Their Pepsis were already warm.

Reymundo and his son, Nahum and his boys. Lorenzo Ortiz, Mario Castillo, Heriberto Baldillo, Efraín Manzano. Abraham Morales Hernandez in sweat pants and running shoes, one of the only guys ready for the marathon. The Guerrero boys, among them a young man named Hilario. Quiet men nobody had ever noticed, many of them nameless—unknown to Mendez, Lauro, or Santos.

They rounded the rock and slipped past a dying saguaro. Their feet crunched on the grit of the desert, and the plants began to tear at their arms and legs. They crossed onto the Devil's Highway on foot. Mendez or Santos did the brush-out: scraped ocotillo and hedionda branches in the dirt to hide their tracks from the Border Patrol.

Don't worry, Mendez promised. Nobody's going to find us.

8

|||||||||

Bad Step at Bluebird

They walked straight up a steep hill. Most of them were in good shape, but it was still brutal. The sand was deep enough that they slid back a half step for every step they climbed and it didn't take long for their thighs to start burning. They were breathing heavily, though to do so this early in the walk seemed a terrible admission of weakness. The older men grimly bent to the task. The youngest didn't even make sport of it. It was a trudge. Many of them breathed through their noses, refusing to gasp, as if not sucking in air would somehow fool the desert into believing they were ready for their ordeal.

Reymundo Sr. helped Reymundo Jr. He climbed beside his son, urging him ahead, telling him to be strong, they only had a few miles to walk. He smiled when the other guys razzed him: Junior was going to be carrying *him* pretty soon. *Cabrones.* Reymundo's brooding brother-in-law, Nahum Landa, no doubt kept his own counsel as he strode into the dusk. He would turn black in the night, invisible except for his eyes and teeth. Reymundo paid scant attention to him, however. His main interest was his son.

Andale, m'ijo. Come on, Son.

Allí voy, 'apá. I'm coming, Dad.

Though it was bad form to complain—machos took discomfort with aplomb—the men did grumble a little. Mendez, though, was no fool. The surest way to beat La Migra was to keep to the high country. No four-wheel drive on earth could cut a drag on a mountain slope or a sheer cliff wall. The peaks and deep ravines were excellent cover, too. Nobody could see them, not even the air spotters. And no Border Patrol unit would bother hiking around hunting them. Their only worries were the passes, where the trucks could drive up. Let the clients complain all they wanted. They climbed.

Night fell.

They topped the hill and dropped into the blue-shadowed valley. Climbed again. On top, Mendez pointed out a red-tipped peak, catching the last light of sunset. "That's the hill," he said. "The second desert is beyond it. We walk through it, and they pick us up." The boys were plopped on the ground, spitting and drinking and murmuring. Ah! There it was! This isn't so bad! Ain't nothin'! They patted each other, laughed. Mendez, like some tractor, geared up and marched away. "Don't rest," he said. "Walk."

Mendez was giving orders to men older than himself. To fathers, grandfathers. The only one younger than him was Reymundo Jr. Even Santos and Lauro, his stooges, were older than him. All he had going for him was his experience.

They were southeast of Ajo. They marched north, and then northeast for ten miles, climbing and dropping, keeping up a good clip. Mendez was a pro—he stormed along, saying little. Later, the survivors would say he gave up speaking altogether. Memories would become deeply unreliable, but they all remembered Mendez, and then Lauro and Santos, whistling in place of conversation. Mendez's loud notes sounded oddly flat against the great landscape. It was a strange scene from some magical novel, the walkers transformed by nightfall into something like birds.

One of the boys, already tired of the Coyotes and their imperious orders, whistled *chinga-tu-madre* (shave-and-a-haircut). Those who heard it laughed.

As they walked, they started to lose themselves. Their accounts of the following days fade into a strange twilight of pain. Names are forgotten. Locations are nebulous, at best, since none of them, not even the Coyotes, even knew where they were. Nameless mountains loomed over them, nameless stars burned mutely overhead, nameless demons gibbered from the nameless canyons.

All ahead of them, beyond Bluebird Pass.

Mendez didn't know it was called Bluebird. He was leading them into a blank map with landmarks etched in transient memory, known by obtuse Coyote descriptions like "The First Desert," "The Second Desert," "The Low Pass," "The High Pass." "The Ajo Lights," "The Highway Water Tank." Bluebird was twenty miles north of El Papalote as the crow flies. But even the crow staggered across that land, taking small detours, unable to ever travel in a straight line.

Their path formed a wide curve that looks, on a map, almost elegant, as if drawn by a protractor. They swerved east, adding three or more miles to their walk. Five miles from Bluebird, they jagged east again, crossed a dead water course that, in time of monsoon rains, might be a foaming little river. But tonight, as the clouds covered the sky, it was a pale strip that made their feet slide and further taxed their calves and thighs.

Mendez had tried to skirt the old trails to avoid the Border Patrol till it was fairly late at night, keeping to high country for much of his walk. Once at Bluebird Pass, he would be able to vector in on the lights of Ajo and hop on Maradona's tried-and-true walking path for the next two nights. He was firmly within the tradition, now: skirt Ajo on the west side, beat it up to the highway and wait for the pickup at the mile marker.

Later, they would remember actually walking through Ajo. Some of them whispered that they passed through a city at night, walked among lights and abandoned buildings on the plain. Empty gas stations standing as if haunted under bright spotlights. "We walked among stores, dark houses."

But this was impossible. This could only be their fevers talking—they never descended onto the town: they crept from crag to peak. And if they were in town, why would they not stop for water or shelter? What midnight mirage did they see? This phantasmagoric town of cold ghostly light and empty streets—where was it? One survivor said it was Phoenix. One of them thought it had no name.

11:30 P.M.

Mendez later claimed that it was all the Border Patrol's fault. The Border Patrol said it was Mendez making up stories. The survivors still have no idea what happened. All they know is that suddenly they were scattered by light.

Mendez later claimed that the Border Patrol was lurking in the hills, waiting for them to come up to Bluebird Pass. It was an ambush, the spotlights like laser beam attacks in a space movie. The walkers stood like deer for a moment, their eyes bright red, their mouths open. They cursed. They shouted.

"La Migra!" Mendez yelled.

Perhaps it was only a Jeep of some sort, making its way up the pass, missing them entirely, but illuminating the hills with its headlights. Some agent out cutting for sign, rolling up the slope to see what was doing at Bluebird. Maybe looking to eat his midnight lunch out of the way.

Lights, nonetheless.

The men scrambled into the dark, running, they thought, for their lives. The lights, Mendez insisted, followed them, chased them into the wilds. And once they were running, whoever it was who lit them up killed the lights and drove away.

Of all the games played along the Devil's Highway, the midnight light game of May 19 is the most mysterious. The Border Patrol's report states: "Sat, May 19, 11:30 P.M. Group arrived at this point and observed lights that they believed to be a Border Patrol Agent at Bluebird Pass." That's it.

But why would Mendez panic if he only thought he saw a Border Patrol agent? He had certainly ducked and hidden from scores of headlights in his career. There was no Border Patrol agent in the world who could make Mendez try to commit suicide—and running headlong into the desert was certainly a suicidal gesture. Mendez never explained further.

Was there a Migra truck climbing into the pass for a quick look? Or were other forces on the land? Were wetback-hunters out, spotlighting illegals for fun? Scattering them before the Border Patrol could get to them? So-called civilian border patrols occasionally launched themselves into these hills, but would they let the walkers go without an entertaining chase, or a satisfying few rounds popped off from a hunting rifle?

If not civilians, then it was the Feds.

Why would the Border Patrol illuminate a large group of walkers and not follow? The Border Patrol regularly spends whole days tracking a single foamer. It is not unimaginable that an agent might be tired, bored, near the end of a shift. He might light a group up and watch them run back to Mexico. Maybe he was scared, which is unlikely—La Migra, like the Coyotes, doesn't waste a lot of time quivering in terror. But if the phantom spotlighter at Bluebird was afraid, he'd call in the cavalry, let the walkers deal with three or four hairy monsters out of Lukeville or Ajo, a couple of Park Service Cactus Cops who don't worry about being culturally sensitive and noncon-frontational.

Illuminating a group of nearly thirty walkers, however, and then letting them go, that wasn't a game any Migra agent would enjoy. No report. No pursuit. No arrest. It simply was not reasonable to assume that this could happen.

Even the Evil Rogue Migra Agent scenario doesn't make sense. An agent attempting to send the walkers to a grisly death, chortling wickedly the whole while, would assume that there would be a rescue attempt. He would know that the next Border Patrol sector would likely detect them, would know that the signcutters would backtrack them right to Bluebird, back to him. Even if they all died, their footprints would tell a story, and that story would ultimately lead them back to him. Besides, there was never a Border Patrol agent in history who would pass up the chance to bust a group of thirty walkers.

The only thing known for certain is that at 11:30, at Bluebird Pass, twenty miles south of Ajo, mystery lights panicked Mendez. Like the totemic rabbit tattooed on his arm, he bolted at record speed. His pollos followed. In their hurry, they dropped their bags, lost hats. They tripped and skinned knees. One of the Guerrero boys, Maximino Hilario, dropped his gallon jug in the scramble and didn't have time to find it.

They scurried up a slope and squatted in the brush and the rocks and waited out the light beams. Ironically, it started to rain. They hunched their shoulders and endured the chill downpour. A few of them cursed the water. Some desert this was.

The lights were gone. The air was moist. Several of them decided the walk really wouldn't be as bad as everybody said—it was, after all, raining already, they were halfway there, and they'd already escaped the Migra. They'd only been walking a couple of hours. Time for m&m's.

"The highway's right over the hill," Mendez said.

It wasn't.

AFTER MIDNIGHT.

They veered northwest in the dark. Mendez allowed few rest stops. No one knew what he was orienteering by—since the rain had started, the stars and moon were hidden behind cloud cover. Even with clouds breaking up, and the sky becoming partially visible, Mendez was hardly a master of the astrolabe. He wouldn't have been able to tell the North Star from Venus.

They didn't know that Mendez was in uncharted territory. He probably knew it, but seemed to think he could work out the puzzle of the landscape. Maybe he thought he was fooling everybody. They didn't know where they were supposed to walk—they'd go where he told them to go. For all they could tell, they were about to drop into Dairy Queen for a milkshake. So he marched ahead, striding with great purpose.

Later, the signcutters read his tracks and called him *Asshole*.

||||||||

The cutters know many things about a person by the nature of his tracks. They learned something about Mendez and his pollos in the days to come. Mendez always walked point, taking the lead as if he knew where he was going. The men shuffled and stumbled along behind him, wandering off path and straggling, but generally moving ahead. The scuffed fans of grit in their tracks suggested moans and curses, sighs and shouts and whispers. Their sign left a cut across the face of the desert like the grooves in an LP record. Their greatest hits were there, in order.

Thin scab of dried urine beside a brittlebush had the spatter sound and the sigh of relief etched in it like bug-sign. The knee scuff where a man fell, and the smeared tracks of the two companions who helped him up, carried echoes of their grunts, and their exhortations, and an embarrassed, muttered gracias. Empty candy wrappers in the bushes told which way the breeze blew, and carried the crunching of teeth and the smell of chocolate. Empty bottles talked of the growing crisis.

Once the trackers got the tread marks of each shoe, they could follow the ever more delirious steps right up to the feet of each dead body. The sign told them much about each man. One thousand steps; fall, scramble; five hundred steps; lie down on the ground and stare at the sky; one thousand steps; sit, fall over, up on knees, crawl, fall, get up one last time.

This guy walked alone the whole time. This guy walked with his brothers. This guy had his arm around his son some of the time: their tracks interwove and braided together as they wandered. This guy tried to eat a cactus.

⌷ ⌷ ⌷ ⌷ ⌷ ⌷ ⌷ ⌷

Then there were his legs. Mendez's left leg had just a little less thrust than his right. It wasn't much, but it was enough. He thought he was going straight. North. But he angled just enough off plumb to head north-northwest as his right leg out-torqued his left.

Signcutters know one secret thing about walkers. They fall into a pattern and seldom break it. Whether it's a mountain or a bush, the walker will cut either left or right and then he or she will tend to repeat this action over and over.

Mendez always cut to the left. Each time he skirted the objects in his path, he drifted west—to the left. Add to that small bit of field math the slight push of his right leg, and you begin to describe an arc. From north to north-northwest to northwest. Barring an interruption, Mendez could have walked in a full circle: west to southwest to south.

He veered.

Into the Growler Mountains, a savage little maze. His men followed. They tried to climb over the peaks and fell back. Then tried again and fell back again. Ajo's lights were blotted out by the Growlers. They walked by stumbling in the pitch black.

Spines. Chollas hooked into their flesh. Whip-slash branches cut their faces, stung their eyes.

Fifteen miles northwest.

If Mendez was worried, he didn't admit it. He told them they had "just a few" miles left to walk. He let them stop. They fell to the ground, squatted, guzzled their water. It was Sunday morning. They had walked about forty miles, most of it in the dark.

Dawn was coming, and with it, a heat wave.

9

||||||||

Killed by the Light

Dawn came gradually to the Sonoran Desert. With the light, the heat started to fill the land. The promise of fire awakened alien noises all around them. Cicadas went off like sirens. Quail in the arroyos made their ghostly whoops. Desert grasshoppers burst into the air with ratcheting machinery roars.

We're lost.

No, we're not.

Mendez says we're not lost.

We are not lost. I know exactly where we are.

Where are we?

We're in the first desert.

The first desert?

There are three deserts. We're in the first.

How far do we have to go?

Not far. It's in the third desert. Just over those hills.

||||||||

Those hills were the Growlers, where they had already been wandering. Now, Mendez judged that they had to climb over.

It was hardly cool. Temperatures had hovered in the low eighties all night. And the deep rock cuts where they had wandered had held the day's heat and radiated all night. By 3:00 A.M. or so—the bug-sign hours—the heat had moved into space and the cool of the stones could set in. The rocks went from oven-hot to feeling about as warm as a human body. This would be the coolest moment for the walkers, though at the time it felt far from chilly. The next few nights would stall at ninety-four or ninety-five, and the days would explode into triple digits.

In the spring, on that Sunday morning, still between Easter and the start of summer, the sunrise was deceptively gentle in its first manifestations. Many mornings in the western desert start like this. An immense stillness, vast as the horizon, yet somehow flat, echoless, leaning against the ear like deafness. It was not as if the sounds of the world had been swallowed by the desert—it was as if the sounds of the world had somehow failed to enter the land.

Dawns offered an astonishment of birds. In the scrub and mesquite hollows, there were more songbirds than could be heard in the Rocky Mountains. Crows, sparrows, mockingbirds. The cactus wren would have been making his small noises as he went about his business. A scintillation of singing and squabbling cut into the silence. Feral parrots might have fluttered greenly across the sky, arguing their way toward Tucson. A hawk riding a thermal sounding his "scree."

The almost cool air hugging the hardpan, not yet ignited by the white flames of the sun, felt blue. It moved slowly with the last stalling breezes of night. Where the predators had made their kills, white down and scattered gray pinfeathers waved like seaweed in a tide. Crickets, wasps, bees. A rusty understory of insectile melody.

Before the heat dropped on their heads, the lost men were drowned in music.

The coming sun was white. The Growler Mountains collected the light and poured it on them like lava.

That heat sizzled at the edges of things, then slammed into them, instant and profound. It opened certain blossoms and closed others. The desert was full of color, though they couldn't see it from the valley where they awoke. The mesquites had small flowers, the prickly pears showed colors in their buds. The last bats sipped their last saguaro nectar. The first hummingbirds swarmed up from Mexico and took their place. The beavertail cacti had half-moon voids chopped into them by the impervious jaws of javelinas, those stink-pigs already nestling in brush and paloverde shadow for their morning snooze.

Rattlesnakes eased from dens and unfurled in the light, soaking up the day's warmth. Tarantulas backed timidly into their burrows. Scorpions wedged themselves in dark crevices.

For some reason, Mendez decided to break with the pattern. Perhaps he really thought they were only a few miles away from their target. If Maradona had been with them, he'd have known the trails better. But Mendez made his third major error that morning. First, he'd gotten started too early, and they'd been precooked by extra hours in the sun. Then, he'd taken the wrong turn at Bluebird. And now, he started walking in the light. As the men followed him again into the Growlers, they had already begun to die.

| | | | | | | | | |

As Melchior Díaz once demonstrated, not only Mexicans die in this desert.

Campers dot the sand at Buttercup Valley in the Imperial Dunes of California. It's just across the river from Yuma, yet part of Yuma sector's patrol area, perhaps one hundred miles from the spot where the twenty-six walkers began their journey. Happy off-roaders sputter and zoom all through the back country. Dirt bikes, ATVs, and dune buggies swarm these dunes. The signcutters leave them in peace, sitting nearby and watching the sky for buzzards, a sure sign that illegals have perished. On that day in May, there were go-carts kicking up rooster tails and VW buggies cutting doughnuts in the sand. White folks in RVs cooked breakfast and watched the *Today* show on their little TV sets.

Jump-cut to late June 2002.

Lisa Scala and Martin Myer went camping at Buttercup. They took their dune buggy along for some backcountry fun. Lisa Scala was twenty-nine years old—a good-looking woman with blond bangs and a warm smile. Martin Myer, forty-two, was recently laid off from the Goodrich Corporation. They probably just wanted to forget their worries for a weekend.

They headed into the desert, no doubt sure that they'd be back in camp in time for a cold one and a grilled hot dog. They hit the dunes and bounced into the land on a beautiful hot day. Neither had taken the recommended two gallons each of drinking water. They didn't need it—they could drive back to the camp in a few minutes. No doubt a cooler full of melting ice sat in the shade under the picnic table. Brewskis, diet sodas. Then a pin jostled loose from the steering arm, and the steering wheel broke off the column. They were suddenly stranded.

Lisa was found a few days later, still sitting in the dune buggy. She died waiting for somebody to come save her. She apparently never got out of her seat.

Martin had tried to walk out. No doubt he told Lisa to wait right there and he'd be back in a matter of hours. A kiss goodbye. A *Don't worry*. Probably even a joke or two—they had been in the dunes a million times. It was their playground.

He made it about two hundred yards.

Later they found Martin lying in the sand. Even with the efforts of the Border Patrol's cutters, and even though he was less than a mile from Lisa, it took them more than two days to locate him. The land tried to hide him and keep him for itself.

That same summer, on July 6, a similar tragedy took place near the eastern end of the Devil's Highway. There, I-8 turns to I-10 and rushes across the south. Past the turn-off is the Rooster Cogburn Ostrich Ranch. (Signs read: "Feed The Ostrich!") As desert distances go, it's a short hop to the Wellton 26's jumping-off point.

Rooster's ostriches scamper around the base of a strange volcanic remnant known as Picacho Peak. Picacho has a kind of cocked-hat appearance, its top slanting at a jaunty angle. It feels like some kind of magic if you're not paying attention, for it moves back and forth across the freeway as you approach it on I-10. First it's on your right, then it's on your left, then it's not there, then it's in front of you. Jet fighters do smoky loop-the-loops out on the vast plains to the starboard side of the freeway. Pale orange dust devils, some of them several stories tall, march through the desert and batter themselves on Picacho's flanks, falling apart in a sprinkle of dirt. From the peak of Picacho, you can see the tips of the Growler and Granite Mountains. That Saturday, the Popielas went for a walk in the park.

In the newspaper pictures, they are extremely charming. Joseph, thirty, is tall, with long hair, glasses, and a beard. His smile is radiant. Laura, twenty-six, his bride, is short and blond, and her hair is curled, and she looks like she might break into laughter at any moment. Joseph was involved in live theater, and they were planning to leave Arizona for Indiana. Perhaps they went to magical Picacho to say farewell.

They didn't carry enough water. Can there ever be enough water? Probably not. But the Popielas carried a couple of those little plastic twenty-ounce bottles with them, the kind you buy cold in the Coke cooler at the Circle K. They might have stopped in Marana, bought some Corn Nuts and a couple of waters and some gum. They listened to the radio on their way, joking and flirting, possibly planning to kiss each other once they walked the three miles to the peak. A six-mile round-trip, with the steady sound of freeway traffic never silent, whispering in the air like a rushing river.

A few hours later, Laura was found dead on the trail by a recreational walker.

Joseph was in sight of their car, parked in the lot. He could see Rooster's rancho below, and a diner featuring soft-serve ice cream cones. He had headed off trail, apparently trying to blaze a shortcut down the hill. Trying to get help for his wife, the cutters assumed.

It couldn't have seemed that hard—perhaps Laura fainted, and Joseph was hurrying down to the car, water, phones, rescue. But he fell on the slope. Hyperthermia will do that to you, make you clumsy. He hit dark rock and never got up.

They went together to the same cold room that had housed the Yuma 14.

In the desert, we are all illegal aliens.

| | | | | | | | |

Experts can't give a definitive schedule of doom. Your own death is largely dictated by factors outside of your control, and beyond accurate prediction. Your own fitness is a factor, your genetics. Gender doesn't seem to affect your chances much. Women are far from being the "weaker" sex. They survive as long as men, and often survive longer. Hydration before the event might buy you time, same with shade, a hat, rest. How much, however, remains unknown. All sources say you will die in a period of time that can vary from hours to days.

However long it takes you to die, you will pass through six known stages of heat death, or hyperthermia, and they are the same for everyone. It doesn't matter what language you speak, or what color your skin. Whether you speed through these stages, or linger at each, hyperthermia will express itself in six ways.

The stages are: Heat Stress, Heat Fatigue, Heat Syncope, Heat Cramps, Heat Exhaustion, and Heat Stroke.

The people most at risk from hyperthermia are the elderly. That's why Midwestern heat waves feature dead Chicago retirees by the score. But the wicked genius of Desolation is that it makes even the young old so that it can kill them more easily.

|||||||

Heat Stress.

Everyone has been tired, or even dizzy, from walking in the heat. Everyone has been sunburned, sometimes quite badly. And many people have suffered the swollen fingers, feeling like sausages, and the funny stumbling at the tail end of a hot hike. This is where it begins. General discomfort, nothing heinous.

A little heat rash. Headache from the glare. Thirst.

The Wellton 26 felt this immediately upon climbing their first hill. They were already tired before they began, perhaps slightly dehydrated from all their journeying and restless sleep. Some of them may have had diarrhea from the bad food and water on their long bus trip. When one of the brothers from Hidalgo said, "This heat is killing me," he was telling the truth.

The heat becomes personal.

|||||||

Heat Fatigue.

As you walk, the relentless heat makes your warm spots wet— your armpits, your crotch. Your head sweats, your neck, your skin blows a fine mist like steam to regulate your heat. You're a big swamp-cooler, with water passing through your membranes and keeping the meltdown at bay. Most of your heat comes out through your head—your head is a chimney. Most of you didn't think to bring a hat. If you're from Mexico, your hair is probably black. The sun encounters body heat on a dark field. Heat wrestles there, rising and descending and meeting itself.

Your scalp burns along the part in your hair, or where your hair is thin. Your cheeks, your neck burn. Your eyelids burn, too. And the tips of your ears. Your lips are not only burned by sun, but by wind; they become dehydrated, and they get rough and flaky, and you keep licking them to try to wet them, and they get sanded until they crack and bleed. Minor trouble.

But you still have water, so you're okay. If you brought beer, you're an idiot, because alcohol makes you thirstier. The ground is burning your feet—it's 120 degrees through the soles of your shoes. If you wore sandals, and many do, you are getting sunburns on the tops of your feet. Hither thither is getting in your sandals and giving you minor burns. You might have blisters—water goes through your system to fill them. And now your jug is getting hot—your drinking water is starting to get as hot as coffee.

The desert's air, like you, is thirsty. It's sucking up your sweat as fast as you can pump it, so fast that you don't even know you're sweating. But you've been walking across rough terrain for a couple of miles now, and you are breathing hard. The air comes to your lips and pulls water from you. Every breath dries out your nose, your sinuses, your mouth, your throat. Your tongue: you drink more hot water; your tongue, you take just one more gulp of hot water; your tongue. Desolation drinks you first in small sips, then in deep gulps.

Your spit turns to paste. Your mouth tastes nasty, so you take another little drink. You tell yourself you'll only sip a couple more times, but to hell with it—you take a big pull off the bottle. Your lungs, now, are leaking moisture to the vampire air. Your tears leak into the sky—eyes dry and scratchy.

The fluid in your lungs helps transport oxygen through the tissues into the blood. Less fluid, less oxygen. You breathe harder, you get drier.

|||||||||

Heat Syncope.

You have a fever, though it's a fever imposed from the outside. Oddly, your skin is getting colder. Your face, even if you're a Mexican mestizo, turns pale.

It gets a little hard to talk. When you go to lick your cracking lips, your tongue is dry and sticky. Words break; you speak in half-consonants, chunks of thought. Your tongue! You would have trouble saying "tongue" at this point. *Lengua*, the word in Spanish, is almost impossible. You talk like a stroke victim.

Your mind is circling a couple of ideas, and you try to use whatever discipline you have: I can take this next step! I can take this next step! This isn't so bad. Just one more sip. Don't gulp. One tiny lil' sip. OK, just one. One more. One more. Suddenly, your hot water is gone. You can't remember where you dropped the jug. Dizzy. Where's the water?

You turn back.

Water's over here. Where. Is. The. Water.

Here?

You circle.

Oh, well. To hell with the water. I'll find water. Water. Water.

You think you're back on track. Where were you going? Follow the leader. You step behind a bush and urinate. Precious fluid and salt quite literally pissing away.

Your heart beats as though you've been running.

You think you'd better take a break.

Where's my water?

Syncope is a noun that denotes *contraction:* in a literary sense, you shorten a word by chopping out letters. Never = ne'er. Ever = e'er. Desolation has begun to edit you. Erase you.

| | | | | | | | |

Heat Cramps.

Now you're officially in trouble. Your body has been dumping salts. Without salts, your muscles can't function. That's why people drink Gatorade.

Muscle cramps kick in. Your legs suddenly ache. You get clumsy. You tumble. When you fall, you hit rocks, cactus, gravel. Your hands are skinned, your knees abraded. A little blood steams away. If you cry, you make an infinitesimal investment in your own death.

Your arms hurt, your calves hurt. Your hands hurt. Your heart can hurt. Your throat clicks when you try to swallow.

Your abdomen clenches on you. You think you have to get to a toilet. If you're a woman, you're having contractions; you think you're going into labor. It's the men's first menstrual cramp. You can't pass that gas. You double over.

Eighty percent of lost walkers can still be saved if the Migra spots them. You can recover with water and an IV. Even the Migra's famous air conditioning could save your life. You could be slumped in the seat with the blower going in your face, a canteen in your lap, and "Highway to Hell" on the FM. But if the Migra doesn't find you, you've stepped onto the lip of the death spiral. Your options for salvation wisp away like steam.

||||||||

Heat Exhaustion.

Your fever is spiking now, and like the flu, you have gotten more and more ill. Headaches. You get nauseous, you want to vomit. If you vomit, you lose more fluids. You are not only clumsy, but enervated. Your body is weak, and your will is slipping. Your tongue is wood. You could give a damn. Your heart pounds, loud in your ears. Your breathing is shallow and fast, and each breath dries you further. Eyelids scrape across eyeballs dry as pebbles.

Your skin is icy; you might shiver.

This is a good place for the infirm among you to have their heart attacks. Your fluid level has dropped—there's not enough fluid to fill the container of your body. Your heart beats faster, trying to suck up some blood from the internal drought. Cardiac arrest hits when the pump overstrains itself and blows up.

Those in good shape will, sooner or later, faint. This is the brain's way of stopping the machine, like hitting the brakes when you realize you're speeding toward a cliff. The body knows. If the brain can stop the body, put it in a little coma for a moment, it can slow the whole process down and regulate organs and try to tend to damage control. Take inventory: Hmm, a little blood in the pancreas, let's move it over to the heart and shoot it up here to me! The brain is all about keeping itself alive. You could go blind and live, have a heart attack and live, lose a kidney and live. But if your brain rots, there's no coming back. It sucks up all the blood and all the oxygen it can get. But it still can't get enough, and it misfires like a dying engine.

First, you get tunnel vision. You might hear echoes. Your body falls on burning ground. You stare through a little hole at the fading world.

You can get second-degree burns from lying too long on the ground. And you sweat, especially where your body forms a seal with the earth. And you breathe. You get up worse than you fell, then you fall again.

And still, you might be saved. But you are now at the borderline, standing before the abyss. One more step, and you cannot return. Another border crossing.

You don't know much anymore. You are confused; your memories are conflated with your dreams. Walkers see demons, see God, see dead relatives and crystal cities. They vomit blood. The only clear thought in your mind now is: I'm thirsty, I'm thirsty . . .

It is maddening. You dream of pools, seas, you dream of a lake and you dream of drinking the whole thing dry as you soak. You'd pay all your money for cold water. You'd trade sex, anything, for water. Walkers who find abandoned vehicles break open the radiators and die from gulping the antifreeze.

|||||||

Sooner or later, you understand that you have to drink your own urine.

You piss in your hands, or in whatever container you might have. You try not to dribble a single drop, and you lament all the priceless piss wasted on the desert floor. You hold your breath and forget the taboos and you gulp your own hot mess. And you piss into your hands again until it's gone. You're alive! You've beat death with your own water!

If you're really lucky, someone might piss in your mouth.

Although nobody drinks it, healer women in Mexico regularly use a thimble full of warm pee in infected ears. Certain insect stings can be treated with fresh urine. Eye infections are sometimes urinated on. Making the leap to drinking your own might not be impossible.

You don't know it, but some of your more enlightened North American brothers are voluntarily imbibing it.

A surprising number of urine home pages can be found on the Internet. Urine is a kind of new-age panacea, and apparently a small dose of the elixir can fight any number of maladies. Urine is a homeopathic wonder drug. A squirt of the fresh stuff contains, according to the Urine Therapy Web site, the following substances:

Alanine, allantoin, amino acids, arginine, ascorbic acid, bicarbonate, biotin, calcium, creatinine, cysteine, DHEA, dopamine, epinephrine, folic acid, glucose, glutamic acid, glycine, inositol, iron, lysine, magnesium, manganese, melatonin, methionine, nitrogen, ornithine, phosphorus, potassium, protein, riboflavin, tryptophan, tyrosine, urea, vitamin B6, vitamin B12, zinc.

People pay good money at their health food stores for DHEA, melatonin, tryptophan. Face creams are full of urea. Pergonal, the fertility drug, is made of human urine. And, as the pro-urine Web sites enthusiastically proclaim: "Take the 'M' out of Murine Eye Drops, and what do you have?"

The village healer, peeing in a *campesino*'s pink eye, is at the cutting edge of medicine.

The recipe for the proper use of urine is:

Collect a midstream sample of fresh (light) urine

Avoid all genital contact, particularly female genitals
⅛ oz. distilled water
Add 1 drop fresh urine

Shake 50 times
1 drop of this solution added to ⅛ oz of 80 proof vodka (as preservative)
3 drops of this mixture under the tongue

But of course, you're lost in the desert. You have no distilled water, or you would have drunk it. No vodka. No eye droppers. You have to gulp full mouthfuls of the pure product.

That first urine is pretty good, as urine goes. It is still relatively clear, since it is the cycling-through of your gallon of drinking water. The first urine is yellow, and if you're lucky, it's pale yellow. The paler, the purer. Pale yellow is the Evian of urine.

The next time through, that same urine has picked up more filtered impurities, and it is a little darker now. Saltier. By the third round, it is orange. It smells bad. Then dark orange. Then pale brown. Then a darker and more poisonous brown. It looks like foaming Guinness stout. By the time your effluent is black, you're doomed—even if you wanted to, you probably couldn't drink it. It stinks of fish. Your body would retch. There is almost more bio-garbage in it than water.

The last stage of hyperthermia begins.

|||||||

Heat Stroke.

Your blood is as low as it can get. Dehydration has reduced all your inner streams to sluggish mudholes. Your heart pumps harder and harder to get fluid and oxygen to your organs. Empty vessels within you collapse. Your sweat runs out.

With no sweat, your body's swamp-cooler breaks. The thermostat goes haywire. You are having a core meltdown.

Your temperature redlines—you hit 105, 106, 108 degrees. Your body panics and dilates all blood capillaries near the surface, hoping to flood your skin with blood to cool it off. You blush. Your eyes turn red: blood vessels burst, and later, the tissue of the whites literally cooks until it goes pink, then a well-done crimson.

Your skin gets terribly sensitive. It hurts, it burns. Your nerves flame. Your blood heats under your skin. Clothing feels like sandpaper.

Some walkers at this point strip nude. Originally, BORSTAR rescuers thought this stripping was a delirious panic, an attempt to cool off at the last minute. But often, the clothing was eerily neat, carefully folded and left in nice little piles beside the corpses. They realized that walkers couldn't stand their nerve-endings being chafed by their clothes. The walkers stripped to get free of the irritation.

Once they're naked, they're surely hallucinating. They dig burrows in the soil, apparently thinking they'll escape the sun. Once underground, of course, they bake like a pig at a luau. Some dive into sand, thinking it's water, and they swim in it until they pass out. They choke to death, their throats filled with rocks and dirt. Cutters can only assume they think they're drinking water.

Your muscles, lacking water, feed on themselves. They break down and start to rot. Once rotting in you, they dump rafts of dying cells into your already sludgy bloodstream.

Proteins are peeling off your dying muscles. Chunks of cooked meat are falling out of your organs, to clog your other organs. The system closes down in a series. Your kidneys, your bladder,

your heart. They jam shut. Stop. Your brain sparks. Out. You're
gone.

|||||||

And the men headed deeper into the desert.

PART THREE

||||||||

IN
DESOLATION

1 0

The Long Walk

SUNDAY, MAY 20—6:00 A.M.

A nd chaos fell upon them.

Their narratives wander like they wandered, their minds unable to process the details of their torments. The rescuers who came to look for them did not know who they were rescuing. The dead were coordinates on topo maps, identified by GPS numbers. They were all collected in the same general subset of coordinates: they were all within a region bound by N. 32/ W. 113. Some of the bodies of the dead were never identified by name. At best, names were given when the survivors identified them later in the wild free-for-all that followed the rescue operation as everyone fell upon the health center in Yuma. Walkers, corpses, Migra, sheriffs, Marines, pilots, BORSTAR operatives, print reporters, EMTs, ministers, Mexican officials, INS officials, coroners, TV crews, radio personalities, consuls, do-gooders.

To this day, some of the dead are only remembered in Wellton Station as "This poor guy," "That poor guy there." The cutters get quiet when they look at the pictures. They just stare at the corpses of the men who died naked.

‖‖‖‖‖‖‖

Walking.

They were deep in the Cabeza Prieta National Wildlife Refuge area. There are several watering spots in the refuge, if Mendez had known where to look. Seven chances to survive. Much would be made of these missed opportunities after the long walk was over.

As the men trudged, their rage grew along with their despair. It was that goddamned Mendez: no, it was this evil desert. No, it was the pinche Mexican government that picked the homeland apart, officials who got fat and rich while they starved. No, it was the Migra, it was the gringos, it was the U.S. government and its racist hatred of good Mexican workingmen just trying to feed their children! They themselves were the fools. The men who talked them into coming, those cabrones, they were the ones. They would get Don Moi for this; they would get El Negro; when they were out of this desert, drinking beer in Phoenix, they were going to put the hurt on Mendez and he would never forget it. Somebody was going to get it! Somebody was going to pay.

Walking.

Desert bighorn sheep no doubt pondered their passage from above. Mendez headed north, now that the sun was up and he could tell what direction he was going. He was clearly aware that Ajo and salvation lay over the unforgiving mountains to his right. He repeatedly tried to climb over the Growlers, dragging the crew up until they foundered, and then fell back, to hit the burning grit and bake as they rested. Then another slog north until a mild-looking slope presented itself, and they tried again, only to be foiled by the heat and the deceptive nature of these desert mountains. Just when they thought they were topping the summit, a higher ridge or peak appeared. The whole time, he was trying to maintain command, to seem in control as control clearly slipped away from him.

One of the men later said, "We'd climb a mountain, and there would be another mountain on top of it."

Another: "They told us to keep going forward, but where were we going to go?"

Mendez was savvy enough to know what the walkers—and perhaps his Coyote partners—did not: if the group didn't get back to Ajo, they would die. His frustration was immense, and it was terrifying. Like hundreds of doomed wanderers before him, he had the tragic understanding that some form of deliverance was just beyond his reach.

He didn't want to die, and a large part of his later defense focused on his efforts to lead the group to safety. His accusers would use the same exact testimony to prove he attempted to kill all of them. It is commonly believed by the Border Patrol that he was trying to save himself. The other men just followed.

They walked about three miles in a straight line, until the land and Mendez's trend toward the left veered them west again. Each rest stop wearied them further as the sun and the soil burned them from above and below. Santos, the chubby Coyote, was far behind Mendez, pushing the stragglers.

By midmorning, they were getting giddy with exhaustion. Even Mendez seems to have gotten confused. His trail wandered deeper west until it suddenly jerked eastward again. He next led them on a zigzag that took them directly northeast for two miles. He clearly thought a canyon ahead would dump them out in the flat land, and he'd be in sight of the familiar peaks beyond the town.

The group, by this point, had no real integrity as a unit. They were tired, thirsty, confused, afraid. They spread out in a lazy scraggly line, some of them staggering and wandering so far behind they didn't even see their comrades. If not for the gulleys where they walked, the land funneling them into the Coyotes' tracks, they might have drifted away into the wasteland and died that day. But they trudged on, sinking deeper into their own miseries as they penetrated deeper into the Growler range. Those who rested, ironically enough, had it harder than those who walked without stopping. It took the resting walkers longer to cover the same distance. Longer struggle in the sun, exhausting rushes to catch up.

José Antonio Bautista: "Wherever my uncle Nahum Landa was going, that's where I was going. We were going there, to the same place. I didn't know where I was going."

Then Mendez entered the gap.

He might have thought he'd gotten to Charlie Bell Pass, which would have spilled him through the Growlers, south of Childs Mountain. He could have headed dead east from Charlie Bell and walked into downtown Ajo and ordered a beer. He had already missed Bluebird Pass. And he had failed to enter a small opening called Temporal Pass. Temporal and Charlie Bell were his last chances to cut back to safety.

But this gap would prove, again, to be a dead end, a nameless indentation in the back range of the Growlers that looked for all intents and purposes like the right pass—a nameless arroyo spilled west out of the canyon, and to the east, Chico Shunie Arroyo had roots in the other side of the high ridge. He was only about five miles off.

Not knowing this, Mendez led the group east, into the new canyon, and they started to hurry a bit, sure that he had finally broken through. Water. Beer. Shade. A ride. Water! And one by one, small group by small group, they staggered to a stop.

Mendez stood and stared at the wall of burning rock between him and the world.

||||||||

Nobody looked at the occasional buzzard that eyed them with its infernal optimism.

Some of the boys were already running out of water. Hilario

had been walking with none at all, begging sips off the others since he lost his gallon jug at Bluebird Pass. His friends in the Guerrero contingent, veterans of the last aborted journey, had thought to bring extra, and they'd hung on to every drop they could. Hilario got some of their water, but what about the rest of the men? Most of the Guerrero boys were blood relatives: they would have to care for each other. They already looked upon their walking companions and saw dead men. But did they have a duty to keep all of Veracruz alive?

The water in the plastic bottles Mendez carried was hot and drinking it was like drinking nothing at all—it was the same temperature as the furnace of burning air around him. He refused to give any of them a drink. If he went down, he insisted, they all went down. They thought he was selfish and cruel. He didn't have time for their opinions. He stared at the mountains some more. Someone was crying.

He sank to the ground—it was hot enough to hurt.

"Let's rest here," he said.

They scattered, looking for shade of any kind. They fell among the rocks and creosote bushes. They crawled under the sketchy shadows under dry mesquites, and they moved around on the hot griddle of the earth as the rolling sun stole their shade every few minutes.

It was noon.

Mendez checked his watch.

He said, "Let's rest till nightfall."

No one knows if Santos or Lauro said anything.

"It's just a few more miles," Mendez told them, but they already understood that he was wrong.

SUNDAY, MAY 20—NIGHT. NINETY-FOUR DEGREES.

When the hell was it going to cool off?

They had decided to wait till midnight. But the hours had

dragged. The dark had remained as hot as the day. Mendez gave up the wait and ordered them to their feet. They were wasting time.

Inexplicably, he made another sudden change, as much of a mystery as the wrong turn he took at Bluebird. He made a forty-five-degree turn to the left (as always, to the left) and marched straight southwest, in the opposite direction from his last march. On the Border Patrol maps, his path forms a perfect inverted *V*. This detour had cost them an extra four to five miles of walking.

Perhaps Mendez was thinking of breaking out of this detour and heading through Temporal Pass. By the time he'd marched for an hour or so, however, the arroyos and gullies dulled his mind. It was all walls. There was no break. He never turned back north.

His sign tells the story of the misfires inside his brain.

|||||||||

They followed the land, now tired enough to only want to flow downhill; nobody was about to climb anything after their failed mountaineering attempts. Desperation was growing. Reymundo and Reymundo Jr. ran out of water. Reymundo Jr.'s black pants had become a torture device, cooking his legs when he was exposed to the light. Father and son dropped their bottles on the trail.

Santos ran out of water. He was out of shape, gasping, cursing under his breath, more frightened than Lauro or Mendez. He wanted a drink. The Guerrero boys didn't have enough to spare.

The group was like a machine breaking down, starting to shake itself apart.

Lorenzo Ortiz Hernandez, a friend of Nahum Landa's, was sick already. He wanted nothing more than to lie down, but he forced himself ahead in the hope of a resting place. Julian Malaga was twenty-four, in good shape, but he was already slipping. His brother-in-law, Rafael Temich, urged him on. They comforted themselves with thoughts of Chamizal, in the Municipio de Huellapan, home—green leaves, clouds, fog, rain. Women. Rivers. Below them, the sea. They were heading toward the great Growler Wash, a dry watercourse that would mock them with its sandy bed. The only possible sources of water in this direction were all dry—Spains Well, White Well, Monreal Well. Even if they'd held water, they were far away, and lost in the wilderness, small blue dots in a vast empty map.

Among them, Hilario, the first to run out of water, managed to march on, his mysterious strength carrying him through his thirst.

|||||||||

Mendez lost what sense of direction he had left. Perhaps it was the exhaustion. Perhaps it was the heat. Once he took them out of the detour, it's as though he surrendered to fate: he gave up all pretense of breaking through the Growlers, and he went straight west. No attempt to cut north or east at all, as if Ajo had suddenly been abandoned. He started a suicidal hike toward Yuma.

He got less than ten miles before his inner compass fell apart completely.

He veered left, as was his tradition. But then, around eight o'clock, he made a radical turn to the south. All of them followed after him like zombies. Each water bottle emptied on the walk, until even Guerrero was dry. Their bottles marked their path in pale plastic that would gradually soften in the heat.

The group's sign was a scatter of slips and trips, falls and minor one-man detours. There was no thinking evident, no reasoning process at all. Mendez walked, and his herd followed. They were now going in the exact opposite direction that they had come. Forming a vast inverted *U* shape twenty miles wide. Mendez clearly had no idea what he was doing.

|||||||||

Sometime during that confused march, the walkers in the rear realized how lost they were. They wanted to quit, but to quit was to die. Perhaps it was Santos who saw the simple solution. They had left tracks. The tracks led, sooner or later, back to Mexico. Mexico! All they had to do was turn around and walk back the way they had come.

It was a long shot. The walk this far had almost killed them. And Mexico was just more desert and thirst. But the walk ahead was *certain* to kill them. And, if they could just get back to Bluebird Pass, they could somehow go in to Ajo, or be found by the Migra. Somebody would find them.

"I want to live!" Santos said.

Who doesn't want to live, *pendejo?*

"Let's go back," Santos insisted. "Let's all just turn around. We can make it. I know we can make it."

Mendez refused.

The walkers who saw this conflict did not know what to do. Although Mendez had clearly gotten them lost, he was the leader. He was in good shape. He was some kind of bigwig *chingón* in the guía group, whereas Santos was a chubby underling, some weak little man they did not respect. Still, he had a point.

You'll die.

They listened to Mendez. It was like choosing a pickup soccer team. Santos led his small mutiny, calling for anyone with the balls to walk back the way they had come. Calling for anyone who wanted to live. He wasn't lying anymore, he was telling the truth: the only sure way through the desert now was to follow their own tracks and try to repair the damage. The was one path, and it led backward.

Accounts vary. Either three or five men stepped up. The Santos team.

I'm going home.

We're almost there, man.

I don't care. I'm going back.

Go.

I will.

Fine. Go.

Santos, expedition leader. They turned around and walked away. Mendez was disgusted with the fat man. He didn't care to watch him walk away. Some of the walkers watched, torn with fear and worry, unsure what they should do. But they weren't quitters. Men didn't quit. *Hombres. Machos. Viva Veracruz. Viva Guerrero.*

Desolation swallowed Santos and his crew.

No trace of them has ever been found.

SUNDAY, MAY 20—9:00 P.M. NINETY DEGREES.

Mendez walked, they followed.

Men were falling behind. Rafael Temich was worried—he'd lost sight of two companions.

"I said, 'Hey, I think we lost two guys back there.' He just said, 'They can suck my cock. Those guys were dumb assholes before they ever came out here. If they're lost, that's their problem. Not mine.'"

Temich wouldn't forget the comment.

The two lost walkers managed to rejoin the group.

They had been walking now for about thirty hours with a short break the night before.

Once again, they stumbled to a stop.

Everything was repeating itself.

They had wandered into another labyrinth of mountains, the Granites. The group looked up in the eerie dark at peaks that could have been the peaks they had walked away from hours ago. Men fell down, crawled on the ground, slammed their faces into the dirt. Cursed. Prayed. They sank into their agonies, silent. Slept the dreamless sleep of the beaten.

Not again.

Where's the fucking rain this time?
"We'll rest," Mendez said.
He collapsed on the ground.
"A few more miles," he said.
Come morning, it would be time to die.

1 1

∣∣∣∣∣∣∣

Their Names

I will never forget the sadness in my nephew's eyes when he looked at me, shedding tears, and I was unable to do anything except to tell him not to die."

∣∣∣∣∣∣∣

José de Jesús Rodriguez was mad: this was his first trip to the United States, and it was going to be his last damned trip if he had anything to say about it.

Enrique Landeros García was thirty years old when he got lost. He'd come from the coffee village of San Pedro Altepepan. He was walking for his wife, Octavia, even though she didn't want him to go. She was a young bride, and he was proud of that—twenty-three years old. And he was walking for his son, Alexis. Alexis had cried, "Daddy, don't go!" But, he said, I want to change our lives. Surely, Octavia would allow him the dignity of trying just once to make things better. But Enrique didn't have the money to pay for the trip. Don Moi was asking 1,739 pesos. Where was he supposed to get that much money? But Don Moi had a way—there was always a way. The Chespiro Network got on the phones and took up a collection: operators were standing by. Enrique nailed a loan, payable upon employment.

Octavia put up a fuss. Enrique didn't know what to do. All he had was a new pair of cowboy boots. What's that to a family? So, on the day he was to jump in a pickup and ride down to Don Moi's bus, he put on his fancy boots and told Octavia he was going to market with the boys, and he'd be home that night.

Once he got to the pickup site, in Martinez de la Torre, he took off the boots and pulled an old pair of sneakers out of his bag. He entrusted his beloved boots to a friend. He asked him to take the boots to Octavia in the morning. She'd understand what he'd done. He didn't make it to Enrique's house for two days. By then, she had already figured it out, but she hoped for the best— maybe he was only drunk, or seeing a friend.

When she saw the boots, she started to cry. She hugged the boots as if they were Enrique himself, and they gave up their smell of leather. Then she told Alexis that Daddy was gone.

| | | | | | | | |

Reyno Bartolo Hernandez was thirty-seven. He was Enrique's *compa* from San Pedro. Coffee farmer. Married for nineteen years to Agustina. Don Moi's operation lent him eighteen hundred dollars. He wore green pants and matching green socks, Agustina's gesture to make sure he looked nice for when he got to his job.

| | | | | | | | |

Another San Pedro paisano was Lorenzo Ortiz Hernandez. He and his wife, Juana, had five children, aged from three to twelve. Juana was thirty-four years old, and she was ready to bear more babies. The others were proud of him for making so many heirs. The kids were deeply into the ages when they needed things, things he couldn't afford for them. If the coffee prices hadn't dropped, they were his own small plantation staff. But no coffee money, no money at all. The other boys were signing up with Moi. He decided to try his luck.

He borrowed seventeen hundred dollars at 15 percent interest.

| | | | | | | |

Reymundo Barreda Maruri was still plugging away with Reymundo Jr. Even though he was fifty-six, the grandpa of the group, he was not going to stop. As hope failed, he had the impetus of saving his boy to drive him. Reymundo Jr. was suffering, flushed, and stumbling. The father held up the son.

At the last minute, his brother Rigoberto had decided not to come along. Well, thank God for that much. Reymundo would be trying to save two lives then. And to think, the last thing he had done right before they left Sonoita was to call his daughter Minerva to tell her everything was great.

Reymundo had once come to the United States to work, but it had been nothing like this. He had worked at a cannery in Ohio, and then done migrant harvesting at a Mississippi ranch. Unlike many of his cohorts, he had been working for wages when Mexico's economic crisis had hit him, working for Coca-Cola, Presidente Fox's old company, when the plant laid off its workers.

And here came Nahum Landa Ortiz. The Ortiz boys and the Hernandez boys and some of the other boys were related in the ten thousand ways men who come from small mountain villages are related. Nahum kept going. He never stopped going.

José Antonio Bautista, Nahum's nephew, was furious. He hated Mendez for the trouble they were in. Later, he would say, "With enchantments and deceptions, they led us."

| | | | | | | |

146 / THE DEVIL'S HIGHWAY

Edgar Adrian Martinez was young, sixteen. He was from Cuautepec, and his girlfriend was named Claudia Reyes. He was walking for her as much for anybody else. His last words to Claudia had been, "I'll work five years and come home and marry you." His father said, "He said . . . 'I just have to get there. I just have to get there.'"

Edgar walked with his uncle, José Isidro Colorado. His god-father, Victor Flores Badillo, walked beside them. As long as they were together, they were sure they could survive the ordeal. They reminded Edgar to think of Claudia.

Edgar had worked with Reymundo at the Coke plant. Perhaps it was Reymundo who put the idea of the walk in his head. Edgar had been paid eight dollars a day to wash and stack returned bottles. When he could augment this salary with picking coffee beans, he made four dollars a day on his days off.

He told his uncle, "I'm going to build Claudia a house."

|||||||

Mario Castillo was a twenty-five-year-old coffee and citrus plantation worker. It was a reasonable thing to imagine a job in Florida, picking more oranges. He was one of the few who had been in the United States illegally in the past. He had lived and worked in Galena, Illinois, for an eight-month stretch. But the pinche INS and the cabrones of the Migra found him out and shipped him home. Home! There was nothing at home.

His wife, Irma Vazquez Landa, was related to Nahum. She waited in Veracruz with two children. They were five and six. Mario dreamed of building them a house and breaking away somewhat from his parents' help. If he could get a small house built, then he hoped to open a tiny bodega, a store where people could buy some of those Cokes the other boys bottled. Some cigarettes, lottery tickets, candy, stamps. Maybe a couple of those scary crime magazines.

Irma could make tortas for the lunch crowds.
He borrowed nineteen hundred dollars for the walk.

| | | | | | | | |

Claudio Marin and Heriberto Tapia and Javier Santillan walked
with Lauro. Javier was falling behind. The heat was melting his
brain. He was slowly going crazy, babbling weird things. They
didn't think he knew where he was or what they were doing.

| | | | | | | | |

Rafael Temich González was a quiet twenty-eight-year-old corn
farmer from Apixtla. He looked severe, almost Aztec or Maya in
his features. But he had an easy smile and was quick to laugh. He
had good manners, and he talked with his hands: when asked a
question he didn't know the answer to, he'd put his hand before
his mouth, palm out, and shrug, "I don't know."

Rafael lived in a thatch-roofed home on a dirt road. You had to
be careful in these grass and palm frond houses—scorpions and
killer banana spiders could fall out of the fronds. Huge tropical
roaches and beetles fell on you in your sleep like warm rain in
some of the infested homes. Small lizards—*cachorras*—ran the
walls, licking up the mosquitoes and slower bugs.

In this hut, Rafael took care of an extended family. Along with
his wife and year-old daughter, he supported his mother, two sisters, and their four daughters. All of them slept together in the
house.

He had gone on ahead of the rest of them, trying to get to relatives in the Carolinas. He took a bus to Mexico City, and another bus to Altar. There, he called his brother in North
Carolina, then tried to get a Coyote. "But nobody wanted to take
us. So we went on to Sonoita." His brother recommended El
Negro, and El Negro's safe house for cheap food and lodging. "I
traveled for about ten days."

| | | | | | | | |

Julian Ambros Malaga could take it. He was a healthy twenty-four-year-old former soldier. He was sure he could handle cross-country forced marches. He was so sure he could take whatever the desert threw at him that he wanted his teenage cousin to join him. The family put a stop to that. He was Rafael Temich's brother-in-law and they had come here together.

Julian wore his favorite good-luck red-striped soccer jersey. He was planning to make money to build cement walls for his mother's house. He was recently married, and he and his wife were expecting a child that October.

His father said Julian had promised to "always behave with respect," and that he would do nothing to cost his father his feelings of pride.

He had a note from his bride in his pocket.

| | | | | | | | |

The crazy González Manzano brothers walked together. Isidro, Mario, Efraín. They were the Hidalgo contingent. Viva Verde Rico! This whole deal was working out badly—hell, they'd been busted, deported, shoved around, and now they were being dragged all over this hellhole desert. By God, they were going to get their damned money back! Still, they walked like men. They'd show these poor Veracruz boys how to walk. All for one.

Mario was heading for Lake Pleasant, Florida. He'd been there before. He couldn't believe it was such a bitch trying to get back.

Javier García was a pip. A compact little fellow with big whiskers and a balding dome, he was a joker. Everything was funny. Even dying seemed funny to him, as long as he wasn't the one dying. "Dead?" he told the sheriffs. "Whew! I saw twenty dead!" He laughed until he cried. He'd stumbled onto the trip—no real plan in mind—after he'd found the men getting ready at the safe house. "I don't know," he said. "There's a million lowlife hotels in Sonoita. I just saw the group and joined in."

Just lucky—it made him giggle.

⁣ ⁣ ⁣ | | | | | | | |

And who was Lauro? Some scrub. Mendez was the closest thing he had to a friend out there, and Mendez didn't even know his real name.

1 2

|||||||

Broken Promise

The long night of Sunday, May 20, convinced even Mendez that they were all going to die. He could no longer tell them that they had a few more miles to go, because even the stupidest among them, even in their worsening states of confusion, each knew they were only going nowhere. They were at the bottom of their southern march, pointed directly at the Mexican border, yet miles away from it. Even if they had walked those miles, they would have died in Mexican wastes. Once he saw the sun come up on Monday morning, Mendez knew there was no hope. Dawn was easy enough: sun is east; keep it on your right side and you're going north. Noon, however, was a daily bafflement. Dusk and darkness were indecipherable.

What happened next is still debated among them. Mendez has told different versions. The survivors tell different versions. The lawyer tells a version, and the Migra tells a version.

|||||||

Mendez called them together.

Or they called Mendez to their meeting.

Mendez told them they were doomed unless he went to get help for them.

Or they told Mendez they were doomed if he did not go find help.

He told them he could make it to water, and possibly to help. It would be better if he went alone: he could move quicker.

No, he took his partner.

All right, then two were better than the big group. Two definitely had a better chance.

Those two chickenshits planned the whole time to book out of there and save their asses.

Or the members of the group told Mendez he had to save them and go alone to find water. And then, at the last second, he said he'd take Lauro.

He was afraid Lauro might die soon without help.

They pressed their money on him and asked him to get water, to get a vehicle and a driver.

Or he demanded money to save them.

Or he extorted money so he'd have funds for himself after he saved himself and left them to die.

They said, "Take all we have."

Or he said, "Give me all you have."

They collected seventy dollars.

They collected ninety dollars.

Or they collected two hundred dollars.

Or he stole three hundred dollars.

The money confuses more than the terrain, more than the hyperthermia. Versions of the dollar amount, and what the dollars implied, never end.

Mendez: "The people asked me and the other guide to go and get water for them, and they donated ninety dollars to us. Actually, they gave it to Lauro. I never touched the money."

U.S. Department of Justice Immigration and Naturalization

Service Report of Investigation, Case Number YUM200105000-002, page two, quotes Rafael Temich:

"The group offered to pay the guides $70.00 U.S. Dollars to bring them water but the guides demanded $200.00 Dollars more. When the two guides started to leave together the group asked one of them to stay with them and not to go. Rafael did not know how much money the group had given the two guides. (. . .) Monday the guides left and never came back."

Francisco Morales Jimenez remembers Mendez asking him, "Got any dollars?"

"No, no," he replied. "I'm only carrying pesos."

"Oh yeah? I'm not going to walk if it's for pesos."

He demanded two hundred dollars.

||||||||

José Antonio Bautista, from the town of Equimite, gave Mendez ten dollars. His uncle Reymundo Barreda Sr. probably had more money on him than the rest of them and he handed sixty dollars over to the Coyotes. Thirty for him and thirty dollars for his already dying son. Bautista recalls a hand reaching into the group and giving Mendez a twenty dollar bill, but he can't remember whose hand it was.

There's the ninety dollars.

Mendez, again: "We never imagined that the temperatures would be so high. So then the illegals asked me and my companion to go for water and they gave us ninety dollars to buy the water, because we didn't have any money on us."

No money. That part is true: guías seldom carried money. Like the bad clothes, the lack of money would serve to disguise them should they be arrested. A guy in new Air Jordans and a Kangol hat, with a roll of Benjamins in his pocket, would be sent on the express train to the holding cell. So Mendez had been broke. But he didn't stay broke for long.

||||||||

The Border Patrol's "Operation Broken Promise" report: "The two guides collected money from the group and told them they were going to get water. They told the group to wait in this location and abandoned the group."

United States Attorney Paul K. Charlton, "Proffer of Factual Basis in the matter of United States of America v. Jesus Lopez-Ramos":

"The group's condition deteriorated dramatically (. . .). The aliens began to consume cactus and their own urine in an attempt to sustain themselves and to fend off the effects of heat exposure and dehydration. As individual members weakened and succumbed, the group splintered into several smaller groups. During the evening of May 21, 2001, several group members demanded that Jesus Lopez-Ramos depart their location in search of water and transportation for those that remained alive. Lopez-Ramos agreed, collected $90.00 from the group's members, then set out with 'Lauro' (. . .) to locate water."

Well, the men say they met at dawn, not evening.

||||||||

The INS official press release reverses this testimonial and has Mendez collecting the money and leaving, and then the group begins to succumb to the heat, to fall apart into disparate groups, and to die.

Mario González remembers: "We hit it and we hit it and we hit it again. When we were all dying, we told them, 'Don't be nasty you assholes. Go get us some water.'"

Maximino Hilario remembers the Coyotes demanding money, but he doesn't know how much. Mario González adds that the walkers did ask Mendez to go for water, but that Mendez rejected all pesos. It was only the long green for Mendez. Francisco Morales says Mendez only collected ninety dollars of that cash, but that he did demand it, and that he put it in his pocket: Lauro never touched it. José Isidro Colorado Huerta saw Mendez take a hundred dollars.

Nobody, then, can agree on how much, or how it was collected, or by whom, or for what reason, or when. The stated purpose was, of course, rescue. Later legal wrangling would focus on the fiendish plot of Mendez. Coyotes always collected the money from their pollos before leaving them to die. They always said they were going for help. They always said they would be back shortly, then failed to return. They always demanded dollars. Why not? They were going to Phoenix to smoke dope and pick up hookers. Pesos would mark them and be beneath the gangsters' level of cool.

What made Mendez different? In the eyes of law enforcement and the prosecutors, there was nothing. Nothing at all. Mendez walked like a duck and quacked like a duck.

For his part, Mendez—if he told the truth—found himself in a *Twilight Zone* episode. The only thing he could argue, forever, was that it wasn't as bad as it looked. All the evidence, all the known history of the region, all the collected cop intelligence on Coyote MO's pointed Mendez out to be a killer. Hey, he said, just this once, all the evidence is wrong.

Whatever happened, for whatever reason, it happened at dawn on May 21.

⌁⌁⌁⌁⌁⌁⌁⌁

One thing was certain: Mendez was getting sick of their bullshit. He was scared, worried, even embarrassed. But he was tired of their insults and their surliness. They called him "asshole." They'd started to buck him, all these older men making him feel like a little kid. Those González brothers—*chinga'o.*

Rafael Temich kept asking, "How much longer?"

All last night, he'd been asking it.

"How much longer?"

"Three hours."

Temich didn't believe him.

The González brothers didn't believe him, either.

I know what I'm doing.

Oh, yeah—you knew what you were doing last week, too. *Pendejo.*

You got us busted, asshole.

I can get you out of here.

Right. Ha ha.

Don't expect us to pay you.

Wait till we tell Negro. Chespiro's going to ream your ass, Rockero-boy!

The other men sneered and snickered when the González clan called him out. Old Reymundo. He yelled at Mendez.

You're killing my son.

I didn't kill anybody. I'm saving you.

Do something!

What do you think I'm doing?

Walking in circles like a *pendejo*, that's what you're doing.

All right, Reymundo Sr. was in a panic over his son. But still, Mendez did not dig it when the old-timer snapped at him like that. What did they think he was, their maid? Mendez was in charge, not these lowlife wetbacks.

He stood there. They stood around him. The meeting, no matter which set of details you choose, had the same outcome:

"How much longer?" Temich demanded.

"Three hours."

"Look, you said three hours last night. We've walked more than three hours, and we're nowhere near a town!"

Mendez shrugged.

"Three more hours, and we're there."

"If it's three hours, then you go. We won't make it."

"It's probably two hours."

Reymundo Sr. blew: "You said it would be right over the mountains. We went over the mountains. We never got there. We won't ever get there. We'll go all night, and morning will come, and we still won't be at the highway. We won't ever get there!"

Rafael Temich says Mendez would only go if they gave him two hundred dollars.

Each dollar bill that went into the Coyotes' pockets was another augmentation of the federal counts that waited, like the mythical cool water, at the far end of the trail.

They gave Lauro a hard time, too.

You'd better come back for us.

Or what?

We'll find you.

Yeah, yeah. Fork it over, man. Talk is cheap.

"I will come back for you," Mendez promised.

Rafael Temich: "I said, 'Why don't one of you go, and the other stay here with us?' And they said, 'No. We'll both go.' We all cooperated. We all gave money because we couldn't stand it anymore."

Once they had pocketed the funds, they told the walkers to wait where they were. All things being equal, if the land were flat and easy, they were approximately fifteen miles north of the Mexican border, twenty miles on a diagonal from where they entered the United States, twenty miles from Ajo, nearly forty miles from I-8. They were buried in the Granite Mountains. But all things were not equal. Surrounding them were the Aguila Mountains, the Mohawk Mountains, the Sierra Pinta, the Bryan Mountains, the Antelope Hills, the Crater Range.

Mendez told them to wait, and he'd be back with water and help. Those with watches checked them.

"I'll be here in five hours," he told them. "Stay here or I won't be able to find you."

"Five hours, right."

"He'll be back in five hours."

"Five hours," Mendez said. "No longer."

Everyone agreed—five hours—they could make it that long.

Some say Mendez and Lauro had a little water; some say they did not.

The men looked for what shade they could find.

Mendez and Lauro marched north.

| | | | | | | |

"We waited."
       —Nahum Landa Ortiz

| | | | | | | |

The day tormented them. Thirst. Pain. Men crawled under creosotes, under the scant shade of scraggly mesquites. It was a dull repetition of the entire walk. As rote as factory work. Their hours clanged by like machines. They were in the dirt like animals.

Six o'clock in the morning took ten hours to become seven o'clock.

A week later, it was eight o'clock.

The temperature screamed into the nineties before nine o'clock.

They waited. They couldn't even talk. They panted like dogs, groaned. Men put their hands to their chests, almost delicately, as if checking their own pulses. But they were barely awake. They were half in dreams and half in the day, and the day itself was a bad dream. Dry wings swished in the air around them. Voices, coughing. Far above, the icy silver chips of airplanes cut the blue. Out of reach.

Ten o'clock.

"Just a little longer."

Their arms were too heavy to lift. They couldn't get their watches up to their eyes. The heat was heavy. The sunlight weighed a thousand pounds.

Their mouths were as dry as the soles of their feet: their tongues were hard and dense and did not want to bend. They sucked and sucked at the insides of their mouths, but they couldn't raise any spit.

Eleven o'clock.

Reymundo Jr. was sick—his body was cooking from within. His father tried to shade him with his body.

"Does anybody have any water? I need water for my boy."

Mendez didn't appear.

Noon: no shadows.

"Where are the pinches Coyotes?"

"Water!"

The temperature was ninety-five degrees in the shade.

Mendez didn't appear.

One o'clock.

Coughing.

Some of them were fainting, melting on the burning gravel.

"I want to go home."

Mendez didn't appear.

A voice cried out: "I don't want to die!"

Two o'clock.

Mendez didn't appear.

"How long are we going to wait?"

It was obvious to some of them that Mendez was never coming back. A few of the boys didn't want to hear it—if Mendez didn't come back, then surely they were doomed. It might have been Nahum who told them if they didn't walk then they were all guaranteed to die. Right there. It was their choice.

Julian Malaga turned to Rafael Temich, his brother-in-law.

"Rafael," he said. "Look, this place is completely desolate. Where are we supposed to walk? We don't know where we're going. Let's wait for the guides to come back."

Rafael Temich says, "But of course, they didn't come back."

They agreed to stick together and walk north. All of them. It had to be north. Mendez had gone north, the bastard, and he was saving himself. They'd follow Mendez.

Once more, the men stood, and they walked.

|||||||||

José de Jesús Rodriguez: "They never came back. Those fuckers left us hanging in that incredible heat."

Now the illegals were cutting for sign.

They walked. They walked. There was no other story: they walked.

They said cholla cactus looked like trees covered in spike balls.

The group started to break apart as the demons and angels started to sing. They could smell their own stench. It was embarrassing. It was frightening.

Nahum Landa Ortiz: "We kept walking. We were walking all day in that fucking desert, going under trees. That's when they started dying. When we got to the trees."

Men stumbled away toward illusions in the brutal light. Men thought they were home, walking into their front doors, hugging their wives, making love. Still, they walked. Men were swimming. Men were killing Mendez. Men were on the beach, collecting shells and watching their children splash. Their women stood naked before them, soft bellies, hands on ribs, breasts. Men hid their faces from a furious God. And they walked.

A voice was heard in the light-shatter, saying, "He's going to die. Lay him down here and let him die. Keep walking."

The desert, out of focus and suddenly terribly sharp, burst white and yellow in their eyes. It tilted. Elongated. It was at an impossible angle! It tipped up toward the sun, and if they didn't crawl, they would slide right off it and fall forever. It made noise: THERE WERE ENGINES BENEATH THE DESERT. It made evil grinding noises, mechanical humming. No, it was insectile, the screech of hunger and derision. The devils were under the rocks, spitting insults. THE BLACK HEAD LAUGHED. I believe in God the father, creator of heaven and earth. No, it did not fucking laugh—it was a silent as a graveyard out there. Just the crunch and slide, crunch and slide, of endless hopeless footsteps. Hundreds of footsteps.

Crunch. Slide. Gasping: that was the sound. Gasping and sobbing and coughing and heartbeats. *Canta y no llores!* The ragged breathing of those walking beside them made the men cringe. Stop to piss: piss in cupped hands, lick every hot smear of it from your fingers. If they weren't trying to save themselves, they would piss in each others' mouths. Sacrament. Communion. Oh God, in Thy dwelling place, hear our pleas. Hearts drumming, soft hammers inside them, dull fuzzy banging, faster and faster. Blessed Mary, Mother of God, pray for us sinners now and in the hour of our death, amen. *El tuca-tuca-tucanazo!* WINGS ABOVE THEM. BLUE MEN. WHITE TEETH. NOTHING. EMPTY NOTHING EMPTY BONES EMPTY HEAT NOTHING BUT SUN EMPTY NOTHING.

IIIIIII

And Mendez and Lauro walked. They were way ahead of the group, making good time. They had hope—if no one else had hope, they did. Go north, man. Go north. The freeway had to be right there. Right there! Water and a ride. It is possible they thought they'd find help for the lost walkers behind them.

But damn, those cabrones lagged! Trying to get that group moving, and moving fast, was impossible. The two of them, even sick, even dizzy, were moving like a race car compared to those slowpokes they left behind.

And why were they behind? Because they were dying. No question of that. It crossed their minds, it had to cross their minds: the walkers were going to be dead by the time they got help, if they got help. By the time they got to Mohawk, got drinks, caught a ride, phoned the Cercas gang, got help, went back. They'd all be dead. What was the point? Mendez and Lauro: they were prepared for the desert, and the walkers were not.

Did they debate it? Did Lauro urge Mendez to just walk away?

Those guys called us assholes! We did all we could. Look at us—
heroes! And if we get caught, then what? Jail? Prison?
Deportation? For a bunch of dead guys?

"Keep walking," Mendez said.

"I am walking," said Lauro.

||||||||

The Trees and the Sun

The men Mendez left behind walked. Five of them climbed a peak to look for lights. There, they saw a lone Migra truck patrolling in the far desert. They ran down the mountain, falling, scraping their hands, but there was no way to reach him.

They made it to some scraggly mesquites. It was a hurricane of sunlight, and like storm victims, the men hugged the hot trunks, clutched the trees to keep out of the killer sun, even tied themselves to the trees. Nahum remembers them going out, one man per tree, the group widening and dispersing as the men sought shade. Each alone, in the awful silence, hanging on with what little strength they had left. And then the gibbering and wailing began.

Francisco Morales: "I don't remember exactly what the days were. But it was in those days, during those days, between Monday and Thursday? When it happened. Monday? Did they start to die on Monday?"

According to the Border Patrol, it had taken the men twelve

hours to walk ten miles. They walked for what few miles they could before nightfall, Monday. Survivors report that about fifteen of the men had thorns in their feet. They had trouble walking, and they were having trouble dealing with the pain of their injuries. Some of the men tried to do healings on the feet of the injured.

With their last vestiges of reason, they decided to set a wildfire. The area they were in had bountiful dried brush, dead grass, creosote, buffel grass, the occasional tumbleweed. They knew enough to remember they were either in, or near, a national park habitat of some sort. They didn't know what it was, but they knew it meant Feds. They thought the little airplanes that maddeningly flickered in the distance might see the fire and call it in.

A couple of the boys were smokers. What they wouldn't give for a cigarette now! A cigarette! With this dry mouth? *Estan locos.* Some could still muster up the energy to bitch and even make small jokes. And the smokers had their little plastic cigarette lighters. *Andale!* Hope was at hand.

Those who could, started to gather kindling.

Reymundo Jr. was desperately ill. He lay in the dirt, cold to the touch and moaning. Edgar Martinez, from Cuautepec, was sick, too. He stared at nothing. Abraham Morales Hernandez, in his black pants, was cooked half to death. His white tennis shoes were like two small ghosts in the scrub. He was fading in and out.

The strong ones got the brush piled up and clicked the lighters a couple of times.

"Come on, cabrón, light!"

A flicker. A flame. It started to burn.

They laughed.

The fire leaped up and out, and they scuttled back from it as it lit up the hillside. Sparks whirled into the sky, blended with the stars. It crackled. It was hot, the one thing they didn't need. But they didn't mind. It was immense and brilliant in the dark! A beacon!

They had saved themselves.

|||||||||

Nobody came.

By dawn, the fires were sputtering, the ash gave up thin ribbons of smoke. They waited. Waiting again. It was all suffering and waiting. Their whole lives.

No airplane veered toward them. No helicopter came. No Migra.

Nahum knew it then. The Guerrero boys knew it. Reymundo Barreda Sr. knew it. They were dead.

They secretly eyed each other, wondering who would be the first to fall. They prayed that they'd live. Or they prayed to die, as long as their brothers, nephews, uncles, sons might live.

TUESDAY, MAY 22.

It was the high spike of the heat wave. The temperatures burned up through the nineties with the sunrise. By midmorning, it was 100 degrees. By noon, 105. By two o'clock, it was 108 degrees.

They walked.

Nahum Landa Ortiz: "I didn't watch the first ones die. Two died apart from us. They were behind us and I didn't see them die."

He says the guides took five men with them when they left. But they didn't. The group was fracturing, and small cells were moving into the landscape on their own. Francisco Morales says, "We started throwing things away. We were going to die. We threw away the things in our pockets in despair."

Edgar Martinez, who didn't have a phone at home, who had to be reached if anyone called through the phone booth in Cuautepec, a village with the name "Hill of the Eagle," middle name Adrian, nephew of José Isidro Colorado, in love with Claudia Reyes, son of Eugenio, stumbled. He righted himself and put out a hand and fell into a bush. He got to his knees, grimaced as if smiling. Perhaps he was ashamed to be falling. He was sixteen years old.

He reached a point registered on GPS coordinates as N. 32.21.85/W. 113.18.93.

He fell again. He closed his eyes. He didn't rise. He lay there for the length of the next day, lost in a delirium no one can even imagine, burning and burning.

| | | | | | | |

Not a mile from Edgar, Abraham Morales tripped and hit the ground. He crawled, rolled on his side, kicked. His eyes were red. He was at N. 32.21.85/W. 113.18.94.

Nobody seemed to know him, for when they finally came and collected his body, he would lie neither claimed nor identified for a month, alone on his icy drawer.

| | | | | | | |

Francisco Morales: "I do not know who was dying or how many because I too was dying."

José de Jesús Rodriguez: "That day, at three in the afternoon, I was dead. What time is it right now—it is four o'clock. Yes, I died. I was dead from three o'clock to four o'clock. I revived and came back from the dead at eleven o'clock at night."

Morales adds: "We were walking like robots."

They could not bury their dead. There is some evidence they didn't know who was dead, since they were all falling and fainting, and those who were awake didn't always know what they were seeing.

They walked three, perhaps four miles farther. Men collapsed. It looked like more deaths were inevitable. Five of them decided to go ahead and see what they could find. Perhaps they'd find Mendez. Or the way. Anything.

"Wait for us," they said, but some of the men were already unconscious, and nobody really said anything to them.

Wait. Hell, they'd already waited.

"When we got sick," José Bautista says, "there was no shade. So I crawled up to hide in the rocks. One of the boys went crazy and started jumping up and down. He started screaming, 'Mama! Mama! I don't want to die!' He ran up to a big cactus and started smashing his face against it. I don't know what his name was."

Nahum and his companions were hiding in the trees.

A voice carried on the still air, crying, "Mother, save me!"

Mario González Manzano and his brother Isidro, far ahead on their attempt to find rescue, watched their brother walk away, in search of escape.

"Somebody said the freeway was right there, right over the hills," he said. "They lied."

Isidro and Mario were in luck: they found some prickly pears—*tuna* in Spanish. "We ate the tunas to stay alive," Mario says.

The liquid in the cactus fruits spared him. He would only see dead bodies when he got to a Border Patrol truck and saw them stacked inside.

|||||||

The sign of the dead could be ghastly and haunting. One of the men tore off his shirt and tried to bury himself. The hither thither he left all around him showed violent kicking and arm flailing, as if he were swimming. He managed to get the top half of his torso buried in the ground, where he either smothered or passed out. The relentless heat baked him, literally cooking him in the ground. His face bloated and came loose from the bones, tender as barbecued pork.

Reymundo Jr. collapsed in his father's arms. Reymundo Sr. held him as he died. Shook him, cried over him. He called for help, but the only thing that might have helped his son was water.

When Reymundo died and slid from his father's arms, his father lurched away into the desert, away from the trees, crying out in despair. Some of the men said he took the American money he had saved for their trip and tore it into small bits.

Julian Ambros Malaga was also said to have torn up his money. His brother-in-law, Rafael Temich, after being prodded by Julian to walk and save himself, was helpless to save him. "That's when he took out his money and started tearing it apart. And he took off alone and I also was demented. I was demented. I couldn't help him. I couldn't carry him. Then he threw himself into the sunlight, and that's where he stayed."

Old Reymundo also threw himself into the sunlight. He was shouting and crying and throwing money into the air, and he walked until he fell, trying to swim in the dirt as if he'd fallen into a cool stream.

|||||||||

Nobody knows the name of the man who took off all his clothes. It was madness, surely. He removed his slacks, folded them, and put them on the ground. Then he took off his underwear, laid it neatly on the pants. He removed his shirt and undershirt and squared them away with the pants. As if he didn't want to leave a mess. His shoes had the socks tucked in them. They were placed on the clothes to keep them from blowing away.

He lay on his back and stared into the sun until he died.

Later, Kenny Smith, from Wellton Station, said, "This poor guy just crossed his ankles and went to sleep."

|||||||||

Nahum Landa's testimony reads like modern poetry:

We were in the trees, trying to hide from the sun.
And they would yell to me, there's a guy dead over here.
And there's a guy dead over here.

There must have been thirty of us out there, and twenty of us
 died.
By Monday we were all dead.
I was hiding under that tree.
Out there, I saw people in despair.
I saw them without water.
I don't know why I survived.
Maybe it's a miracle.
Some of them just died of desperation.
Some of them went insane.
Some of them lost their minds.
You could hear them screaming.
Some fell all alone.
I heard one guy screaming, daring the Border Patrol to come
 find him.
Stupid things like that.
He was desperate.
He started singing.
We were drinking urine.
We were ripping open cactus.
Some of the boys were saying you could cut the thirst with a
 cactus.
The majority of them died that day.
I was going to die this morning.
I have spines from these pinches cactuses all over me.

1 4

‖‖‖‖‖‖

Helicopters

Mendez and Lauro stumbled. Lauro was sick. He kept muttering that he couldn't go on. No, man, Mendez told him. No way—you're not dying now. We're there. We're *there*. Can't you see?

And they were there. In desert terms, they were right on the back porch of salvation. On high points and rises, they could actually see the Mohawk peaks. It was incredible, what they'd done. From the valley where they'd left their pollos, they had walked forty miles. It was a major accomplishment—merit badge stuff, Eagle Scout–quality marathon hiking. Considering the condition they were in when they started, it seems almost impossible that they made it so far so fast.

I can't, Lauro kept crying.

You can.

I can't!

You can!

Mohawk meant freeway, and freeway meant rest area, and rest

area meant water and Cokes and Mars bars and rides and even the pinche Migra. Being arrested by the Migra—oh yes, that seemed like a really good deal right then.

You can make it.

But Lauro couldn't.

He fell down.

I'm going to rest . . . right here . . . right under . . . this lit-tle . . . tree.

Mendez tried to wake him, to get him up. Mendez got down on his knees and shook him. Slapped him. Lauro only snuffled and moaned, as if he were dreaming some sweet dream.

Mendez took the money from his pockets, what money Lauro had. Then he tried to get up. Was astonished to find that he couldn't stand. He pushed on the ground, but his legs gave out on him.

How about that?

Those damned legs.

He grabbed bushes and tugged and rose a few inches and fell over. The twigs ripped across his palms.

Ouch.

He got on his knees.

That hurts.

Okay.

All right.

All right, fine. I can do this.

The freeway's just over there.

No problem.

He started to crawl. He went on all fours, and sometimes he went on his knees like a religious penitent. The world of sin and grace spun in flaming disks around his head. He fell. He rose. He lay. He crawled. He tried to rise. He sat down.

He thought it would be a really really good idea if he just lay down right over here under this little bush for a minute and collected his thoughts. He slumped, he fell sideways.

Just a minute.

The coma came up from the ground and covered him.
Celia? I'll get up in just a minute.
Sleep.

WEDNESDAY, MAY 23.

Somehow, it became the next day.

Late in the night, more men had fallen, and the small commando group headed out, five of them, led by Mario González Manzano and his brothers, Efraín and Isidro. With them, young Francisco Morales Jimenez. They made the final dash for salvation.

"My brother was talking about water, water," Mario says. "The five of us said we were going to make it. We were hoping the Border Patrol would see us."

The five men stumbled, sunstruck, down the mountains. They were facing Barry Goldwater Range. Efraín broke away. The Border Patrol report states that he became ill and they left him behind. The brothers say he went up a mountain to see what he could see. He was too weak to come down and died up there.

Mario: "We went to the cactuses finally and broke them open to try to get water out of them. We had walked very far. We were dying. There wasn't even a tree where we were. The heat was sitting down on us and we were dying. We were looking for the Border Patrol because we were dying. We were looking to the right and the left for La Migra because we were dying."

West and north, the vast bombing range sprawled. In its heart, there were false villages with empty houses—ghostly curtains blowing from empty windows. These are strafing targets, and the signcutters regularly have to roust sleeping illegals from the hollow living rooms lest the fighter bombers blow them away. And deeper still, huge tractor tires are arranged in rings and painted red and white, echoes of the tires wired together to pull the drags. Illegals often sleep in these, too, not knowing they are bomb targets.

To the south, the Cabeza Prieta wilderness, the Pinacate Lava Flow, the Devil's Highway. Ahead: the Lechuguilla Desert, the Copper Mountains, Raven's Butte, Tinajas Altas Mountains, Coyote Peak, the Wellton Hills, the Gilas. And to the north, Mendez, sleeping under a bush, Lauro slowly dying in his wake. Beyond them, the Holy Grail: I-8. And Wellton Station, where Kenny Smith half-listened to the radio in his back room, and Ol' José, the grinning skull, smiled down from the wall. And coming south from home base, agent Mike F. made his way down the landscape, cutting the drags, rattling over the bumps, looking for fresh sign, checking the hiding places.

And then he saw them.

||||||||

Mario, after he could speak, after Mike F. gave him water, told the American his brother was lost in the hills.

Mike called in the Banzai Run.

At home base, the Trailer Trash uttered their famous "Oh, shit."

Vehicles from all sections of the sector responded.

Mike F. cut sign back into the hills, searching for the lost González Manzano brother, Efraín. It is important to note that within ten minutes of finding the lost men, the Migra was already fully engaged in rescue. Mike F. found Efraín at GPS position N. 32.24.40/W. 113.22.53. It was too late to save him. Agent F. reported it: "One male, deceased." Efraín was in sight of the Mohawk Valley and the freeway, if he'd known where to look. Like many of the walkers, Efraín was in love: his sunburned arm revealed a tattoo that said "María."

While Mike F. cut for more sign, the old boys were kicking off their desert race. The Border Patrol sped there so fast, with so many vehicles, over such vicious terrain, that they suffered twenty-six flat tires. Some agents drove on rims to get there.

Marine pilot Major Robert Lack took the call that morning

and scrambled. He flew over Mike F. and the lost walkers and circled the rough terrain. His crew spotted bodies scattered on the
ground, and he landed among them. Ten men were on the
ground, and one was dead. They were in their underwear. When
the crew dragged the men into the choppers, they were too tired
or weak to sit in the seats. They collapsed on the floor and went
to sleep.

Altogether, five helicopters joined in the hunt.

I I I I I I I I

Reyno Bartolo. N. 32.23.16/W. 113.19.55. Face up, green pants,
green socks. Deceased.

Enrique Landeros. N. 32.23.17/W. 113.19.54. Blue underpants. Deceased.

José Isidro Colorado felt death catching up to him. It was a
force that came from outside him. He tried to outwalk it, but it
was faster, stronger than he. He stumbled. He thought it was no
use to fight any longer—the battle was finished. Death caught
his clothing, and he started to fall asleep as he walked, knowing
he would fall and never awaken.

Then he heard his daughter's voice. She was calling to him
from somewhere nearby. "Papi! Papi!" she yelled. He opened his
eyes, looked around. "You promised to build us a house!"

José got up off his knees—how did he get on his knees?—and
walked again. Until he was spotted.

Agent Blaine Wilson led the Tucson BORSTAR units by air.
Agent Stuart Goodrich, Migra pilot, took to the air and began
cutting the drags from the air. The sheriffs joined in: Yuma's
Ralph Ogden took to the hills. He said, "It was dirt, some rock,
just a few small trees." BLM ranger Ruben Conde helped find a
group.

It was a mobilization worthy of a small invasion.

I I I I I I I I

Abraham Morales Hernandez. N. 32.21.85/W. 113.18.94. Deceased.

The rescued thought they were dreaming. Heriberto Baldillo Tapia might have awakened long enough to think he was saved. The cutters got him off the ground and into a chopper. As they tried to get a saline IV into him, and the helicopter rose and turned west, Heriberto cracked his eyes. He might have seen the helicopter crew. His eyes rolled and drifted closed and he died.

Nahum Landa said he wanted them to forget giving him a drink—he wanted them to pour cold water over his head. The sound of helicopters filled the sky, the calls of Migra agents. In spite of their terrible situation, it was still tempting to hide for a few of them. Even then, they didn't want to give up.

Lorenzo Ortiz Hernandez lay as if asleep beside an ancient saguaro. The cactus was easily three hundred years old, and it had seen walkers die before. GPS N. 32.23.18/W. 113.19.59. Lorenzo was on his back, his eyes open to his enemy, the sun. His brown slacks were empty looking: his abdomen had fallen in, his pelvis held up the material of the slacks as if his slacks were a circus tent coming loose from its poles.

It was 110 degrees before noon.

|||||||

N. 32.13.16/W. 113.19.51. Claudio Alejandro Marin. Black pants, horse head belt buckle. One small mirror in his pocket.

Cutters, Marines, cops, EMTs, rangers, hunted all night. Mendez slept through it all. They cut his sign from the group's breakup point all the way to the outskirts of Dateland. Among their traces were a couple of bottles, which suggests they did have some water.

Lauro was found dead beneath his bush.

When they found Mendez, they thought he, too, was dead. They dragged him out and got him in the helicopter. He might have thought he was still in his strange dream, dark goggles and engine scream, the sky above and the killer dirt so far below.

| | | | | | | | |

N. 32. 23. 17/ W. 113.19.45. Arnulfo Baldilla Flores. His white shirt still looked remarkably clean. His white shoes were scuffed. He had a wad of pesos in his pocket, money Mendez had refused to accept. He had a letter from somebody in his pocket, but out of respect, the cutters didn't read it.

Reymundo Sr. was found at N. 32.23.16/W. 113.19.52. He wore maroon pants and his favorite spur belt buckle. His shoes were gone. Oddly, he only wore one sock. It was black. His son, young Reymundo, was picked up at N. 32.23.19/W. 113.19.56. The cutters wouldn't know until Nahum told them that they were father and son.

The helicopters. Their engines whopped the air. They looked like dragonflies.

Mario Castillo Fernandez wore blue jeans. His belt buckle had a rooster inlaid in the silver. N. 32.23.16/W. 113.19.54. Deceased.

Far back, far east from all the action, Edgar Adrian Martinez lay, still alive, still breathing. It was incredible that he'd lasted that long.

He'd been lying in the heat for days. The rescuers did what they could for him, but he was in bad shape. They called in the coordinates on him and waited for the dust-off to get there. He never responded to questions, they tried to pour water between his split lips.

It must have been his sixteen-year-old body that kept him alive.

Finally, the helicopter came over the peaks. It hove into view and circled.

Edgar opened his eyes. They were dull. Maybe he saw, maybe

he didn't. The big beast hovered over them, kicking up dust. It started to descend.

Edgar raised his head. He opened his mouth, but the motors were too loud for anyone to hear anything. He raised his hands as the machine landed.

He put his head down.

He died.

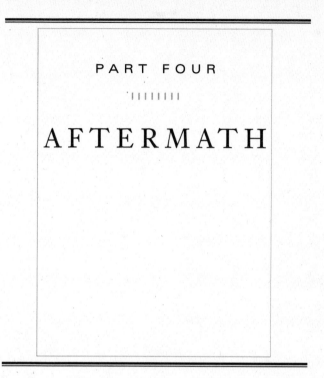

PART FOUR

|||||||||

AFTERMATH

1 5

IIIIIIII

Aftermath

The Border Patrol, enacting a long-standing federal plan, tried to palm the survivors off on the hospital in Yuma without arresting them. If an illegal was brought in and turned over for lifesaving purposes, and the Migra had not officially arrested the culprit, the bill immediately was the hospital's problem. If the clients were prisoners, the government had to pay for their health care. It was not uncommon for illegals to rehydrate, catch a nap, eat some hospital food, then walk out the doors and into the United States. Migra-as-Coyote. But it saved the government money. Seventy-seven hospitals throughout the American Southwest were losing about $190 million in unpaid bills, and tens of millions of these could be attributed to medical attention for illegals, including those dropped off by the Border Patrol.

Pima County, home of Tucson sector, wrote off $24.7 million in 2000 alone. San Diego and El Paso were, incredibly, worse. In Tucson itself, University Medical Center lost an estimated $6.5

million for treatment of "undocumented entrants." And little old Yuma, population 160,000, spent $4.1 million. About a quarter of these bills were from illegals, though the media laid it all on them.

A survey conducted by Florida's MGT of America, a consulting firm, estimated that illegals made up 23 percent of unpaid bills in the Southwest's ER's and care centers. Twenty-three percent might seem like a moderate percentage of the cost—after all, that means that 77 percent of the bills are unpaid by good Americans. Still, elder care, certain emergency services, and long-term care for American citizens were forced to shut down all over Arizona as the toll mounted.

The walkers lay in beds, unaware that they were costing anything.

The border makes number crunchers go mad. It's harder to cross, so there are more Coyotes; the numbers of crossers, in spite of $5.5 billion spent to stop them, keep swelling; deaths increase; wildlife is endangered; landscape is ruined; and supply and demand rule—Coyotes charge more every year, and because of this, fewer Mexicans are willing to return to Mexico. Why risk it? Now that the average cost of crossing is somewhere around seven hundred dollars, only 38 percent of illegals choose to go back after two years in the United States. They simply can't afford to go home.

The lost walkers lay on crisp white sheets, rolled through swinging doors, blinked at confusing lights and masked faces, hospital gowns, the smell of disinfectant and their own strange musky stench. Needles. Liquids. A sign flashed by: THIS WAY HEART CENTER. People in green inserted electric thermometers in their ears. Hands in rubber gloves. "Are we contagious?" one of them asked, but no one answered.

| | | | | | | | |

On that last morning of the long walk, Wednesday, May 23, when agent Mike F. found the men on the Vidrios Drag, it was ten in the morning. The men began to arrive in the Yuma Medical Center within hours. They were met by Dr. David Haynes and his team. It was overwhelming: body after body, patient after patient. Dr. Haynes jumped to it. All of them had kidney damage from the relentless cooking. The Border Patrol and other rescuers were truly racing the clock: Haynes told the local newspaper, "They would all be dead if they hadn't been brought in to the hospital when they were." Later, Haynes told reporters, "Have you ever seen a mummy from ancient Egypt? That gives you an idea. They looked shriveled up."

Nine of them were in fair condition. Two were in serious condition. One was critical. When Mendez arrived, he scrunched low in his bed and tried not to make eye contact. Would the boys cover for him? Would they let him escape?

The walkers went into rooms, sometimes together, and sometimes paired with strangers. Hilario, who had lost his water the first night, not only survived but managed to somehow look dapper in his bed. His hair was neatly combed, and his thin moustache looked like it was drawn on his lip.

Rafael Temich ended up in a room with an old white man. His nurse was named Jenny, and Jenny came and went, wrestling mightily with the old man.

"Did they come and exercise you?"

"What?"

Rafael didn't understand a word of it.

"Who turned down your bed today?"

"Huh? What?"

Rafael kept finding dry little things in his nose and mouth, kept picking them out while Jenny struggled with his neighbor.

"You pulled out your needle!"

"I did?" the old man replied.

"He pulled out his IV."

"What?"

The old man launched loud, hacking coughs into the room.

"Our friend," Rafael said, "is in bad shape."

The hospital's social worker spoke Spanish. He stepped into the room, interrupting the sheriff's interrogation. Rafael's mother called from Veracruz, trying to see if he was alive. The hospital was going to provide him with a call back to her once the cops were done with him.

Rafael said thank you, but he did not smile.

| | | | | | | | |

By 11:30 A.M. that same Tuesday, Rita Vargas was on the case. A strong woman with movie-star looks, Vargas was the Mexican consul in Calexico. Her husband, Felipe Cuellar, was the consul of San Diego. They were uniquely qualified to understand the vagaries of migration and tragedy along the line, overseeing between them the region encompassing the Tijuana, Mexicali, and San Luis migratory corridors. Having originally come from Mexico City, Vargas had made it her business to become an expert in the norteño territories, a land alien to her.

The Calexico consul had responsibility for Yuma (and, by extension, Wellton), which at that time had no consulate. Yuma called Calexico to tell them there were dead Mexicans in the field. Rita Vargas was on the telephone in minutes, hunting down Mexican authorities all over the world.

Rita was known as a no-nonsense consul who brooked no foolishness. While charming and funny, endearing when it was appropriate, she was not afraid to stand up to both the Border Patrol and her superiors. She lived in a world far removed from the decencies of La Capital—no exquisite dining or Aztec collections in Calexico, no waiters in tuxedos with perfect manners, all-night bookstores, concerts and strolling mariachis in Garibaldi, no metro, no small white lights in the trees of Coyoacán where coffee shops served demitasse cups across the street from Frida Kahlo's house. Rita Vargas lived in a world of gangsters and Coyotes, cops and victims. She traded now in mummified bodies and gunshot wounds, fear and force.

In a notorious case earlier in her tenure at the consulate, Vargas handled the case of a classic border shooting. A green Migra agent had fired into a crowd of illegals in the dusty night near Mexicali. He claimed that he'd fired his weapon in self-defense—the gang had outnumbered him and rushed him. One of the runners was mortally wounded. The others, according to his report, turned tail and fled.

While this agent awaited medical evac for his victim, the Mexican slowly bled into the soil. The agent, clearly distraught, turned in his report, and he was supported by the testimony of the old boys of Calexico Station. The shooting was ruled righteous, and the newbie was cleared of any charges.

Only Rita Vargas thought it was worthwhile to investigate the ballistics. A quick review of the coroner's report demonstrated that the wound had entered the runner's back. It occurred to her that a self-defense shooting should have hit the victim in the chest, unless the Mexicans were assaulting the Migra boy with their buttocks. Her investigation sought out the illegals now safely hidden in Mexico. The science and their testimony revealed exactly the reverse of the Migra's report. They had been running for the border, going back. The agent, allegedly young and nervous, had fired at them as they hit the fence, and the victim was hit as he tried to repatriate posthaste.

Vargas famously walked into the station chief's office with her report and said, "Your men are lying to you."

Thus started a respectful relationship between them. While perhaps not a friendship, their mutual respect was a feature of the Mexicali/Calexico corridor during her tenure there. Vargas became close to the chief's wife, for example, and she oversaw the amazing development of a Mexican government service window in the Border Patrol station with his mute blessing.

By 11:30 A.M. of that last day, Rita Vargas already knew that the walkers were mostly from Veracruz. She tracked down the governor of that state at his hotel in Europe. She stopped his vacation cold and gave him a long-distance report. She then pulled her superior out of an important meeting in Mexico City. That work done, she sped to Yuma, where the first of the walkers were arriving by Marine and BORSTAR helicopters.

|||||||||

The men were gawking with huge black eyes at the hustling gringos. Cops everywhere. Huge Migra monsters lurched around them. Deadly serious Latino sheriffs descended on them. Soldiers. Nurses. Pilots. Chaplains. Doctors. The Mexicans soon joined in: scary Federales with notebooks and expensive after-shave lotion pulled chairs up to their beds. *Who did this? Where is he? Where's El Negro? Where's Don Moi? Do you know Daniel Cercas?*

The overwhelming flow of panicky radio calls had been picked up by scanners all over the southland. The scanners started to attract reporters. TV crews sped to Yuma from central Arizona and California, newspaper stringers and borderland beat reporters hustled to the medical center. It was lights and mikes, notebooks and flashbulbs. Television vans raised their satellite dishes. Press credentials flashed in the sun. The hustle and jiggle overtook the parking lot of the medical clinic. Signcutters suddenly became perimeter security experts.

"We're famous," somebody said.

Gringos giving orders—one of the boys thought this was the funniest thing he'd ever seen in his damned life. His arms were full of bloody cactus punctures, and his balding head was burned bright red. But Jesus Christ! He was alive! It was so funny, he couldn't stop giggling. And these cops! These ridiculous cops strutting around. He could have wet himself, they were making him laugh so much. He wiped and wiped the blood that started seeping out of his wounds the more he drank. Pinches gringos! "We're all fucking dead!" he told the cops. "We all died!" He burst out laughing. Showed them the blood. "Death!" It was the best laugh he'd ever had.

The boys were coming in: Rafael Temich, Nahum Landa. They were hydrated and made comfortable. The helicopter racket came through the walls. They stared dully as IV needles were stuck in their veins. As they drank, they started to be able to urinate again, and women held strange little pitchers to the ends of their penises and collected the dark fluid and whisked it away to peer at it in stark rooms. The men were still so stunned by the walk that they weren't able to completely process this unexpected North American development: white women clutching their privates.

Cops stared at them, tried to intimidate them with badges and big chests. Officers who spoke Spanish, some better than others, glared down at them. They set up video cameras on tripods and held clipboards. They had big guns on their belts. Mustaches. Pens. It was all dreamy and stupid. Cops didn't scare anybody. Some of the survivors resented the questions. Some of them were still insane from the walk. Some, like Nahum, went opaque and shifty, not sure what they should say. How much could they share? Any reasonably tough guy from Mexico knew that you were nebulous with cops, and you didn't rat out your associates. Besides, who were these big men? More Migra? Would they deport everybody? Nahum kept his eyes hooded and answered their questions with quiet evasion, with maddeningly impressionistic answers.

"It was the guy with the forelock," he said. "The rooster hair. He left us."

Some of the boys in beds nearby glanced at each other. Everybody was listening to everybody else. Nahum set the course for some of the younger guys: he wasn't going to crack. They wouldn't crack, either. But he sure as hell was going to finger Mendez. Nobody was going to stand up for that asshole. They wanted to help. They wanted to know who was alive. And they were afraid to know who had died. Everything in their lives was chaos and fear. They had only been in the norte for less than two weeks. They still didn't know where they were, didn't know what "Yuma" was—Mexican or American—didn't know if they were going to jail or being deported or if El Negro and Chespiro would hunt down their wives and mothers and kill them.

The beds were comfortable, though. The AC was cool. The Jell-O was tasty. If only the cops would go away and let them get some sleep, things would be a lot better.

But the cops weren't going away.

"Tell us about the rooster guy."

They called him Mendez.

"Did the rooster guy threaten you?"

No.

"Were there any sexual improprieties, any violent acts?"

Sex! No.

"What's the name of the guy with the red haircut?"

Don't know his name. Mendez.

"Is the guy here? The rooster boy?"

I don't know. Is he here? I think he's over there.

And they all looked down the way. Mendez. Oh yes, they said. He's here. He's down at the end of the ward. In that bed. That's the guy with the hair.

And the sheriffs, smelling their prey, gradually made their way to him, recording each survivor as they went, building their case as they closed the distance between them and him. Every few minutes of tape brought Mendez closer to a life in prison.

| | | | | | | |

Rita Vargas arrived in Yuma and started caring for the men. She observed the police interrogations, making sure the survivors knew their rights. She hounded the Mexican pols on her cell phone, called Tucson and told them to get ready for bodies— many bodies. She shook Migra hands and Marine pilots' hands.

She comforted brothers and nephews and godsons. If she could have teleported from room to room, hall to hall, officer to officer, and corpse to corpse, life would have been simpler.

The boys in the beds were all under arrest, so their medical bills were at least no longer in play. The Border Patrol posted a guard on each room, and the guards stood watch the entire time. There wasn't much to be done for the walkers, once the questions had been asked and the reporters banned and the governments of Veracruz and Hidalgo notified. These boys were going to be pumped full of water and antibiotics and saline solution, and then they were going to Phoenix, to some holding cells, somewhere, but they were not going back to Mexico. Not yet. They might get the ol' Migra bus ride to Nogales or Sonoita, kicked off at Lukeville crossing with a stern finger-wag, but not yet. No, we had something cooking here. We had Rooster Boy, and he'd killed—well, nobody knew yet how many he'd killed. But the dude was clearly some kind of Coyote Charlie Manson. He was a monster. He was the ur-Coyote shitheel we'd been hunting for thirty years, the killer of walkers, the smuggler punk. And he'd killed his last freaking load of tonks, that was for goddamned sure, and we had rooms full of wits! We had bed after bed full of witnesses for the prosecution. This was Arizona, man. He wasn't going to get off with a slap on the wrist in Arizona! Lil' Rooster Boy was going to be deep fried and served up. One of the Yuma sector cutters said, "He shoulda stayed home."

So the tonks were going to lie there nice and cool, eating macaroni and Hamburger Helper, sipping OJ and slurping pudding. Then they were going to get in nice big BP trucks and sing their songs. The survivors were suddenly paid professional narrators. At the beginning of their federal jobs, they were paid in room and board. They got cheap shoes and pants. T-shirts. As they sang, they learned they could get job advancement. Even a substantial raise. Like all good bards, they embellished and expanded their narratives. As long as they told their stories, they stayed. As long as they stayed, they had a chance to stay longer. Soon, they would surely earn money.

It was the new millennium's edition of the American Dream.

|||||||||

Paul K. Charlton, the United States attorney for the District of Arizona, was going to take Mendez down. In documents after document in the matter of *United States of America v. Jesús Lopez Ramos*, he righteously flayed Rooster Boy.

"First, the very attempt by the defendant to guide a group of twenty or more individuals through a remote area of desert, on foot, at a time when temperatures were greater than 100 degrees, is, in and of itself, a reckless act. The defendant had been apprehended on seven prior occasions in this area with groups of people. (. . .) Six of those apprehensions occurred during 'summer' months, so the defendant was familiar with the area and aware of the potential for soaring temperatures. The defendant's past apprehensions at various locations in this particular area support a finding that he knew of the vastness of this desert area. On the other hand, the victims knew only what the defendant and his co-conspirators told them: that the walk would take no more than two days to complete, that they would walk at night and rest during the day, and that they should bring an amount of water that they could carry to sustain them for 1 and ½ days. . . ."

|||||||||

Mendez wrote his sad letter, but it could not stand against Charlton's language and organization.

By way of this letter, I ask forgiveness and pardon for what happened in the Arizona desert, because I really am sorry from the bottom of my heart for what happened and it honestly wasn't my intention to lead those people to their deaths. Rather, my intention was to help

them cross the border. But we never imagined the tragedy would hap-
pen. I want you to know that since my childhood my parents have al-
ways been of very low economical resources. My parents had to make
great efforts just to feed us each day. I was forced to leave school be-
cause they didn't have enough economic means to send all four of us
children to school. So I decided to leave my family and look for work,
and make some good money to help my family make ends meet and
buy them a house, since they don't own their own home. I worked le-
gitimately at a factory making roof tiles in Nogales, Sonora. The
wages were truly very low, and that was my reason for getting in-
volved in the smuggling business. I met Daniel at the factory where
I was working and he asked me if I'd work for him by crossing over
illegals and he promised me good wages. I didn't want to, but in the
end I decided to, since it didn't include killing or robbing anybody.
That was why I began to work for him and there were always three
of us guides and I swear, nothing like this tragedy had ever happened
to us before. It was never our intention to abandon them, but rather
to help them, because when three people from the group decided not to
continue and turn themselves in, one of the guides stayed with them,
and if the rest would have decided not to continue we would have all
turned ourselves in. But they decided to keep walking in order to
make it to our destination and I never forced them to keep going. So
we kept on walking, but within a few hours we all ran out of water.
We never imagined the temperatures would be so high. So then the
illegals asked me and my companion to go for water and they gave us
ninety dollars to buy the water, because we didn't have any money on
us. But it was not our intention to abandon them, but rather to help
them. But since the temperatures were so high, my companion died
and I was left very weak and I couldn't continue on to bring help and
if immigration hadn't found me in time I too would have died, and in
my state I wasn't aware of what had happened to the other people. It
was in the hospital that they informed me that many people had died.
I felt very sad and I honestly am very sorry for the family members
and victims and I am so sorry because it wasn't my intention to lead
them to their death. I ask forgiveness and pardon from the judge and

the state for what happened. I ask from the bottom of my heart not to judge me so unfairly, because what happened was an accident and not intentional. I promise not to bring illegals across anymore and I am truly repentant, and ask the judge's pardon and forgiveness.

Thank you,
Jesús Lopez Ramos

| | | | | | | | |

"The defendant's reckless conduct continued throughout this crossing attempt. (. . .) [The surviving victims] repeatedly asked the defendant how much further they would be required to walk. The defendant repeatedly advised them that they were within one to two hours of their destination, and urged them to continue. By his own admission, the defendant had previously guided groups of aliens through the same area of the desert for profit. Consequently, it must have become apparent to the defendant that the path was unfamiliar or that he had taken the group in a different direction than what he had planned. Yet, he never confessed to the members of the group that they were lost.

"The defendant maintains that any member of the group could have turned around and returned to Mexico at any point. However, by withholding the truth from the group members about their situation, even when asked about the same, the defendant deprived them of the opportunity to make any sort of informed decision about whether to continue onward or attempt to return to Mexico. (. . .) This conduct is certainly as reckless as attempting to cross the border with an alien in the trunk of a car. The inherent risks of this undertaking were foreseeable to the defendant."

| | | | | | | | |

The dead bodies, dense and dark, were zipped into bags and delivered to the loading docks. They were shipped to Tucson because in Tucson, the medical examiners had their labs. Rita Vargas joined them. Fourteen dead men on their long drive through the desert. They took up a lot of room, and they weighed a lot. They could be set on vertical racks like big loaves of bread, since they were dead. Still, it took more than one vehicle to move them.

What a lot of bother. This kind of fuss didn't sit well with working men from Veracruz. They didn't like handouts from anybody, and they would have walked back to Tucson and the border if they could have. This flashing of lights, slamming of doors, driving in convoys—it was unseemly.

The vehicles were cool, especially after their terrible days in the sun. The ride was smooth, speedy. The procession of vehicles sped out of Yuma and headed east, out through the mountains and down into the Mohawk Valley. They passed under the silent Wellton Station, where the battered trucks and flat-tire SUVs were still limping in. They flew past the Mohawk rest area, where other walkers no doubt observed their passing from the shadows without knowing who they were. Distant Migra helicopters and small planes flew search patterns, looking like small black birds. The spot where Lauro died and Mendez fell was not five miles from the fourteen as they floated over the road.

It was relaxed. They got to lie on their backs the whole way. No sun hit them. The insides of the bags were fairly pleasant, since there were no major bloody wounds to make them slick or sticky. The smell was already getting nasty, but the heavy rubber kept it from escaping and being humiliating. Mexicans can't bear to be embarrassed by such things as bad smells coming from their bodies. These men had been impeccable in their grooming, as humble men from the interior almost always prove to be.

They went through the small barrier of the ABC mountains, and they skirted the northern edge of the bombing range. Thirty-five miles away, the Devil's Highway baked and coughed up its dust devils. They went along I-8 as if they were in a dream, one of those strange flying dreams, silent and cold. They skirted the north end of the Granites, where they had died. And they cut down onto I-10, their original destination, north of the Papago lands, north of Ajo, cutting across the top of the Growlers. The vehicles made good time on the freeway. The entire trip that had killed them was a matter of a couple of hours now.

The cost of using the vehicles, the drivers, the crews, the gas, was more than they could have earned in a month. But there was no worry now, no thought. Just rest. Down, past Picacho Peak, past Rooster Cogburn's ostrich farm, past the half-hidden CIA jetport and the ruins of a big development in the sand. Sewage treatment ponds cast up brown shit-fountains as if they were saluting them. Traffic parted. Tucson glittered and glimmered. Weird urban statues filled the town: Pancho Villa, a half-buried satellite dish with bronze vultures on it, a giant Gila monster in a traffic island. Out in the far end of town, the eerie airplane graveyard, where hundreds of bombers and jet fighters, helicopters and transports, waited forever on the gravel, home of ghosts and black widows, moaning in the desert wind. Down into town, down the ramp into the coroner's building, down the cement walkways into the cold rooms.

Reymundo Sr. would likely have preferred to have been in the same bag as his boy, but they were kept apart. Reymundo Jr. was alone, lost and small inside the bag, almost swimming in all that black rubber space, sliding around as they drove, and now on the icy metal table. They could have torn the rubber and held hands, but they were resigned to their fates.

Heriberto Baldillo's cactus punctures didn't hurt. Lorenzo Ortiz Hernandez wore brown pants. Reyno Bartolo wore green socks to match his green pants. Mario Castillo Fernandez had his favorite silver rooster belt buckle. Enrique Landeros's teeth were broken, but they no longer bothered him. Julian Ambros Malaga still had his colored piece of paper in his pocket that nobody would ever read. Claudio Alejandro Marin had a small mirror in his pocket, and if he could have, he would have checked his hair one last time. Arnulfo Baldilla had a letter in his pants pocket— he had carried it through the entire ordeal, and now it was safely stored away. They'd had to call a booth in Cuautepec and hope somebody who knew Edgar Martinez would answer. Abraham Morales took the long truck drive with no name—he would lie in a drawer for a month, waiting for somebody to recognize him. Efraín Manzano loved a girl named Maria, and her name was inked into the skin on his arm. Lauro rode, forlorn and anonymous, forever lost. No one would ever figure out his true name, and after a futile search for next of kin, he would go into the soil of the potter's field in Tucson nameless, there to lie, forgotten.

They were close, after what they'd been through. For a brief time, they were all together. It was a silent reunion as they lay in a row, almost touching.

The dead men were loose now. Their feet bobbled when the carts bumped into each other as they were lined up, like they were tapping their feet, or waking up. Most of their eyes were open. Small sounds escaped from a couple of the bodies as gases moved through them. Almost sighs. Rustlings in their bags. If you listened, you could hear them whispering.

We're going home.

||||||||

Home

The living men had a restless night, full of bad dreams. But their exhaustion overwhelmed them. One by one, they fell asleep. Crisp sheets. Pillows.

Presidente Vicente Fox sent as his representative the poet Juan Hernandez. He had a pointy beard, and he was the first Mexican chief of Migratory Affairs. The men looked up at him as he was photographed talking to them. He told them they were heroes of the republic. They weren't used to meeting poets.

The guards watched over Mendez with the tenderness of law enforcement agents who have hold of valuable prey. He lay in the bed, staring into the dark. He knew his life was already over. He was only nineteen, almost as young as Reymundo Jr. No prayer, no mental screams to his mother, to Maradona, or to his Celia in Sonoita, could save him now.

He'd gone down like a macho. He didn't give up anything or anyone. He told them how he'd fallen, how poor old Lauro had fallen. He was helpful in those parts of the story because that's what he was like—helpful. He wanted somebody to see that he was a good guy. Maybe, you know, he'd done something bad, but he was not bad. He almost died! Trying to save these poor guys! He didn't want to hurt anybody, but nobody believed him.

When they pushed him about his associates, about El Negro and Chespiro, about Don Moi and El Moreno, he shut his mouth. They couldn't sweat him, no matter what they did. Hey, they were gringos—no way were they going to do the kind of things to him the Mexican cops and the Federales would have done. Every Mexican gangster knows this—Los Yunaites is the land of human rights, three squares, trials, lawyers. Nobody has pliers or drowning tubs like the Judiciales. Or the Mexican army, with its dank underground cells and its bare electric wires. Gringos could not make Mendez confess. It wasn't going to happen. He was a gangster, and he was going to show them what he was made of. And he knew that El Negro would know, somehow, everything he said. Sixty-seven Altar Street was easy to find. His Celia would be lying there in her white panties, fanning herself in the heat, when they came for her. They'd take her out into the desert, or to someone's garage. They'd make sure Mendez knew exactly what had befallen her.

There was nothing. Nothing. It was the bleakest night of his life, emptier even than the nights lost in the desert. At least out there, he could keep walking. But if he got up now, if his handcuffs would allow him to rise, the cops would shoot him down like a dog.

There was no angel for Jesús Lopez Ramos.

The raised bars of his hospital bed looked like the bars of a jail cell.

| | | | | | | |

The Calexico consulate was authorized to pay for the analysis of each corpse. After the medical examiner had determined that they had, in fact, died of exposure and hyperthermia, after they'd confirmed there were no bullet wounds, knife wounds, signs of blunt trauma, sexual assault, the fourteen men were given back to her care. She had them hauled to the funeral home, where they received nominal prep work. The cost for each man was over a thousand dollars. Plus the cost of the coffins and the shipping trays. The death details had cost about twenty-five thousand dollars. And they still had to go home.

Vargas arranged for a jetliner to collect them. Aero Mexico rented the governor of Veracruz a 727 cargo jet, and it made a special dead-head flight to Tucson. Vargas stayed in a local hotel on her own credit card. In the morning, they collected the dead in another small flotilla of vehicles and quietly took them to the airfield.

It was May 31—a mere week since the men were collected by the cutters. Less than two weeks since they had left home with Don Moi. The procession of hearses cut through Tucson, and people saw them off—an outpouring of public grief that startled everyone there. Church leaders and their flocks, Chicanos, Mexican families, college students, Humane Borders activists and Derechos Humanos warriors, reporters, Anglos, cops, regular citizens—they stood in the heat and watched the twelve go by. Two remained behind, unidentified.

The newspapers reported a "lone bicyclist . . . near Reid Park" standing with his helmet in his hand, head bowed.

A Mexican man attending the procession with his family said, "We just feel for them, and we want to show them that they are not alone."

Raquel Rubio Goldsmith, a tireless crusader for border reforms and more humane treatment of the undocumented: "There should be no such thing as an illegal person on this planet."

The boys had never been in a parade.

||||||||

Each coffin was hauled aboard the plane and secured. They formed a double row in the hold. Vargas was seated in the cockpit of the jet, on the jump seat. Told to keep quiet when they were taking off and landing, but that she could chat with the crew once they were in flight. She was advised to stay out of the cargo bay.

The flight took off without incident, and vectored east, then arced south, cutting over the mountains south of Tucson, crossing the border east of Nogales, closer to the Texas border. The wild landscape of northern Mexico fell away below them like a fractured plate of granite. Blue canyons and red deserts. Pines on the Sonoran and Chihuahuan peaks like black dots.

The dead were taking their first airplane trip. For a short time, they followed their old road trip in reverse, cutting down into the heart of Mexico. The plane skirted Mexico City and its great smoky plateau to the east. By the time they got far south, the sun was setting.

Rita Vargas caught her breath—the dark was spilling out of the mountains as the sun vanished in the west. The deep purple/blue shadows spread out on the water of the Caribe. The ocean was shadowy, yet at the same time, glowing. The massif of the Veracruz Mountains formed a wall that burned electric green on one side, and velvety black on the other. And below, the lights of the cities scattered and burned, white, yellow, white, looking like gems. Stars.

She still recalls it as one of the most beautiful sights she'd ever witnessed, as if the coast of Veracruz were somehow welcoming its sons home. It would have astounded the dead if they could have looked out the windows. Why would they ever have left such a beautiful home for the dry bones and spikes of the desert? If they could have seen what she saw, they might have stayed home.

The plane banked sharply, and Vargas felt the vertigo of watching the land rush at her through the windshield. And then they were on the ground. The engines were roaring as the plane braked, and they rolled ahead, turned, started to drive to the terminals. There, she saw the crowds.

|||||||

Veracruz had already created a public relations mega-event out of the return of their martyred heroes.

The governor himself stood prominently before the seething public. Soldiers and cops held them back. Reporters—all levels of reporter—struggled to get to the head of the line. Famous television talking heads from Mexico City elbowed local newspaper photographers aside. Children held banners, flags. Bands played. Very photogenic.

Fourteen hearses and ambulances stood portentously in a long row, ready to take the heroes to their eternal rest.

When Rita Vargas stepped down the ladder, Governor Alemán began his speech.

"These were men pursuing a dream," he cried.

Vargas tried to face the crowd, but the people surged in a kind of bloodlust or panic, and the metal barriers that the government had set up to separate them from the dead collapsed. It was a scene out of a deadly rock concert disaster—The Who Play Veracruz—and Vargas was knocked down and crushed beneath the weight of the shoving humans. Police and soldiers beat and shoved their way through the tangle of arms and necks to pry her loose from certain death. They dragged her out onto the tarmac, where she caught her breath and stood up, tried to gather herself and straighten her clothes. The governor was already making pronouncements. Commentators were already jabbering: America was to blame! The governor was sad, yet honored, to welcome back the sons of the state.

Vargas watched as each coffin was carried from the plane to great tumult. One by one, they were laid inside the waiting hearses. The doors slammed, and the cars peeled away and sped off, in a big hurry, into the night.

She asked to see the families. The Mexicans led her into a passenger lounge inside the main building. The government had arranged for a photogenic young woman to step forward for the cameras. Vargas was bemused. The grieving families were kept back while the young woman recited a prepared document.

Every moment of the arrival had been stage managed.

Tired, disgusted, Vargas withdrew to a hotel. But she couldn't sleep. She wandered the room, lay on the bed, paced. Finally, she gave up and called for a taxi. She found a last-minute flight back to the United States.

Later, she calculated that the dead men's flight alone had cost over sixty-eight thousand dollars.

"What if," she asked, "somebody had simply invested that amount in their villages to begin with?"

|||||||

The survivors began their ping-pong journey through the system. Mendez, mute and surly in the eyes of the cops, went to jail in Phoenix. He was parked in a six-by-nine cell. Hoots and curses, clangs and stench, industrial paint, steel, cement, slippers, jail suits, gang-bangers, bad food, noise, lightbulbs in iron cages. You crapped near your bunk and slept in your own smell. He watched black men, exotic creatures. Listened to the babbling of Inglés. Radios.

Gerald Williams, his defender, came to see him and started trying to construct a defense. Williams, a veteran of the public defender system, was a dapper African American. This no doubt was of great interest to Mendez.

But Mendez was still playing it all close to the vest. When the consular agents of the Mexican government arrived to interview him, he was unwilling to give them information. He stonewalled their questions. His only enthusiasm was when he asked them to contact his mother in Guadalajara.

His reticence did not endear him to the Mexicans—they did not find his mother for him.

Williams tried to construct a case. Small bits of the story came out. Celia, the bad night at Bluebird Pass, extremely reluctant acknowledgments that there was a guy named Negro, but everybody knew that. Still, Williams was eager for anything, any handle to get a grip on the case. Bluebird Pass! That sounded good. He tried it out: the Border Patrol lit 'em up and sent 'em scattering. Later, when fat Santos vanished with his walkers, there was some suggestion that the wicked BP had caught them, but no one had any record of it. This could be a rich bit of leverage— what if the same evil Migra agents who recklessly precipitated the tragedy had also been the ones who apprehended the guys heading home? They picked up the walkers and somehow sent them over the border without any paperwork whatsoever. Evidence, if true, of wrongdoing, perhaps criminal intent. It was a long shot, but it was something.

Later, Williams heard about the brushfire the boys had started. How unlikely was it that the roving Border Patrol pilots and signcutters missed the initial big group, then missed a raging fire in a protected wilderness? Were there no rangers spotting for grass fires? Was there no Migra agent scanning the landscape? If they saw a fire out there, would they not call it in, to someone, anyone? And wouldn't it stand to reason that a chopper would cruise by, just to see if the valuable habitat was about to explode in a conflagration? Bighorns and Gila monsters and javelinas and saguaros going up in bursts of sparks and billows of smoke? Yet nobody saw it. Or, better yet, if they saw it, they didn't bother to investigate.

A vast borderland conspiracy was at work.

| | | | | | | | |

Mendez liked the direction it was going. He liked pinning it all on the pinche Migra, because the Migra was laying it all on him. Case after case of manslaughter, maybe even murder if anybody could be turned to say that he'd beat them or threatened them. And then there was the detail that troubled everybody except the prosecutors and the Border Patrol: Mendez and Lauro collecting money from the dying.

Any signcutter will tell you that in every case, without exception, when the walkers are abandoned to die by their Coyotes, the Coyotes "borrow" or steal all their money. This is a standard business practice among those who leave humans to die for convenience' sake.

Mendez swore, to anyone who would listen, to Williams, to the jailers, in writing and out loud, that he had set out to save the dying men.

Why did he need money to save them?

To buy water!

All their money?

To buy money and to pay for a ride!

What about every other group left to die? It's a standard lie told by the troops of all the El Negros and Chespiros who work the line. We're going for help; we're buying a car; we're going for food and water; we're hiring a driver. By nightfall, the Coyotes are buying marijuana and hookers with the money of the dead. What about that?

Mendez could only say, "I am not like that."

When the Wellton gang heard this, some of them laughed out loud.

||||||||

The living talked.

Details poured out of them, and cops and the Migra and the prosecutors and the Mexicans listened. Rita Vargas penned a long, detailed report covering every aspect of the event and the identities of the walkers, living and dead. Investigators started hunting down the Cercas gang's U.S. operators. Dark rumors started floating, that the dreaded BORTAC commandos were in

Mexico, on search and destroy missions. An unprecedented wave of investigation was launched in Mexico. Eight hundred Federales were said to have flooded the northland, attacking Sonoita, hunting in Veracruz and Hidalgo. Cercas gang associates started to go down.

Indicted in absentia by a grand jury in Phoenix in September 2002, El Negro, taking his role as a norteño-music-style outlaw seriously, fled the border. He hit the road in his pickup, all cowboy boots and evil whiskers. El Negro wore shades! El Negro drove fast! Women flocked to El Negro! He was sighted all over Mexico. El Negro—the new Dillinger! He taunted them from tabloids. He was reported to have gone, in a dazzling bit of bandido hubris, to Veracruz itself. He was photographed playing soccer, perhaps on the very fields where Reymundo Jr. had once played. El Negro wears shorts! El Negro shoots—he scores! Goal!

Even the newsmen said: This hombre has cojones.

El Negro, in a headline: "Come and get me!"

A Cactus Cop in Arizona who may or may not be involved in BORTAC operations took the news calmly.

"Don't sweat it," he said. "He's cooked."

| | | | | | | |

Associated Press, November 3, 2001: "A man who brought a group of illegal immigrants across the U.S.-Mexican border, leading 14 of them to their deaths in the southern Arizona desert, pleaded guilty Thursday to 25 smuggling counts. Jesús Lopez Ramos, a 20-year-old Mexican national from Guadalajara, had been scheduled to go on trial Nov. 6 but changed his plea during a hearing before U.S. District Judge Susan R. Bolton. A federal jury on May 28 indicted Lopez Ramos on 14 counts of illegal immigrant smuggling that resulted in death and on 11 counts of illegal immigrant smuggling that resulted in serious bodily injury. . . ."

Each count carried a maximum penalty of death or life imprisonment, five years supervised probation after that, and a fine of up to $250,000. Mendez might not have been a great guide, but he was a survivor.

It was a move that startled everyone, including Gerald Williams. Mendez had woken up near the morning of his trial and pled guilty to all counts. His offer was simple: if you don't kill me, I'll admit to the whole thing. Mendez was taken away, not to see the light of day for at least sixteen years. But sixteen years, man, it beat being executed fourteen times.

He had sat out his birthday in jail. He had lost touch with Celia, with his mother, with Maradona. He had seen the evil anniversary of his disaster come and go.

There was no life left for Mendez, and he knew it. His luck had never been all that good. Even in his high times as a gangster, he'd been busted over and over again. The angry walkers in his lost group were right: he was an asshole. Did he believe he had a shot at a successful outcome in Arizona?

He folded.

||||||||

The survivors had played the game brilliantly. They bucked up, and in the face of their grief, their rage, their horror, they stuck together. They had lost family members and friends. They had seen things they could never find the words to explain. They were hurt and scared, physically damaged, perhaps psychically damaged as well. But they were not stupid.

In trade for their testimony, they were rewarded with immunity. The U.S. government plays by these rules: if you have something to offer, you can stay. The American taxpayer saw to it that Nahum and his boys got to stay in Phoenix; they moved into an apartment building together; they were given gainful employment. One government official promised they "would never have to work in the hot sun" and they were found jobs in a refrigerated meat-packing plant, where they grind cows into ham-burger. The effects of their ordeal in the desert have not abated. Rita Vargas reports that one of the men sustained nerve damage to his extremities. He's a hazard to himself at work, since he can't always tell if he's about to cut off his fingers or not. One terrible day, he was cooking, and he put his hand on the griddle. He didn't notice it frying until everybody smelled the stink.

The other guys are hoping to get him home.

|||||||

Since that May of 2001, the filth and depravity of the border churns ahead in a parade of horrors. The slaughtered dead turn to leather on the Devil's Highway, and their brothers and sisters rot to sludge tucked in car trunks and sealed in railroad cars. The big beasts and the little predators continue to feed on the poor and innocent. Hope began to glimmer for a short period as presidents Fox and Bush courted each other. A kind of border accord loomed, and the sacrifice of the Yuma 14 helped stir the leaders of each nation to pity.

Fox had wisely approached the United States in a fresh manner—not with hand-wringing, not with accusations and uncomfortable cries about human dignity and human rights, but with the promise of big profits. He message was clear: Mexico represents billions of dollars in profit. Washington was moved to wonder, *Border? What border?* Sweeping change was coming over the horizon.

But the atrocities of 9/11 killed Border Perestroika. An open border suddenly seemed like an act of war, or a flagrant display of foolishness. The United States was gunning for bad guys.

At the same time, our vaunted trade agreements couldn't penetrate Mexico, couldn't overwhelm the hopes of minimum wage, all the burgers you can eat, color TV, and what looks like free health care. The businessmen and women who run the *maquiladoras* (internationally owned and operated Mexican factories) that were to transform the border have found more, and cheaper (it didn't seem possible) labor in China. By 2002, four hundred *maquiladoras* had shut down in Mexico with more slated for doom. The Mexican paper *La Opinión* reacted with this head-line: "ANOTHER INSULT—Now the Chinese Are Taking Our Jobs." Anti-immigration buffs will appreciate the ironic echo of the complaint.

Just when it seemed like there couldn't be any more people left in Mexico to cross the border, new waves surged. The Coyote operations expanded. As the onslaught swelled, the Border Patrol thinned.

After 9/11, over three hundred Border Patrol agents fled the service and became air marshals, riding in planes for a living with their .40 cal automatics tucked under their arms, watching for terrorists and hijackers over the tops of their *Maxim* magazines. The quip was: *Life sucks, then you join the air marshals.*

At the same time, the American Right demanded more Migra. The INS took direct missile fire for its boggling of the Arab Threat and the collapse of the Mexican border. The old boys of Wellton Station kept driving into the desert, every day of the year. Foamers, wets, walkers, Coyotes, OTMs, and now Arabs. Homeland Security, that long arm of the Fatherland, moved to absorb the Border Patrol into itself, recombining federal agen-cies and trying to forge a colossus of border enforcement.

The cutters themselves reacted with a strange lack of grati-tude: the move cut them off from their union representation. Hardly a bunch of pinkos, the officers in the field still felt they needed fraternal support. Rumors began to fly almost immedi-ately that a substantial percentage of the cutters would flee the new King-Size Homeland border forces.

One of the signcutters smiled when asked about al Qaeda.

"Well," he said. "They're from desert countries. But they're not from this desert. They wouldn't get too far."

||||||||

Today, thousands of maquiladora workers, many of them strangers to Tijuana, Mexicali, Juarez, Matamoros, wake up to find themselves without money in an inhospitable region far from home, where the cost of living is higher, and the padlocked doors of the maquis are echoed by closures and failures all along the line. When Vicks VapoRub comes from a Mexican plant, and your cassette tape and VCR are assembled by an "Oaxaca" who can't read, and the big boys take their Learjets and martinis to Beijing, taking their little blue bottles and their Mylar and circuits with them, it becomes the duty of El Norte's businesses to take up the slack. If only burgers could be cooked in Africa and teleported! If only toilets would scrub themselves, pants stitch themselves, tuna can themselves, lawns mow themselves! If only robots would slice the throats of cows and grind them into sausage! If only tomatoes and oranges and apples, and cotton, and sugar cane, and peaches, and cherries could be harvested by monkeys! If only we had clones! If only wildcat construction projects would frame and roof and shingle themselves!

If only Mexico paid workers a decent wage.

In Iowa City, Omaha, Nutley, Waycross, Metairie, those who survive the northern passage can earn in an hour what it took a long day's work in radioactive chemical Mexican sludge to earn before. The green hills of eastern Arkansas are ripe with chicken plucking factories, and the woods are now alive with Mexican "Templos del Evangelio"—crazy backyard churches not unlike the Sonoita Bible temple down the street from the legendary El Negro's compound. Signs that once said "Jesus or Hell" now say "Cristo o Muerte!" The Oaxacas rush to the Arkansas hills to make a stand against the devious angels of Desolation.

Mexicans still behind the barbed wire continue to listen to fabulous tales of Los Estados Unidos. They watch drunk and disorderly teens vomit in the streets of Spring-Break-Atlán. They wait tables and mop floors while sailors scream and naked girls dangle from balconies. Topless gringas pout on their beaches, where they are not welcome unless they're sweeping up cigarette butts or carrying trays of day-glo liquor concoctions. They watch television, go to open-air twelfth-run movie houses where the tickets cost fifty centavos and the mosquitoes bite their necks. Radio is alive with propaganda: Eminem! 'NSync! Britney! Ja Rule! (They call him: Ha!) It's Radio Free Mexico, on every AM and FM dial! They buy castoff American clothes at the segundas, and by God, even the gringo trash is better than anything else they can buy!

Border dwellers, come from the hinterland, are twelve hundred miles from home but five miles from the United States.

We gonna get it back.

          | | | | | | | |

In ancient days, the Rain God was fed by the tears of the innocent. For any rain to fall now, it will take gallons of tears, rivers. In the desert, the drops evaporate before they hit the ground. Our dead men opened the gate for the most deadly seasons ever seen on the border.

The Mexican consul in Tucson said, "The media only cares about the Yuma 14 because of the large numbers. But this tragedy goes on every day. It never stops. If only one person dies out there, it is exactly the same horror story."

Victims are continually gutted by the power. In Juarez, young women are still being slaughtered and abandoned in desert lots, rotting and mummifying where their rapists and torturers dropped them. Their empty chest cavities are home to bees and scorpions. No one knows yet who is killing the women. All they know is that more than three hundred of them have been butchered. A reporter from Mexico City who went to Juarez to investigate was abducted and beaten so severely that he was permanently disfigured. Local women's rights groups whisper that it's "Los Juniors," the pampered sons of the maquiladora owners, engaging in sport with the easy prey of poor displaced women. Cops say it's Satanists, or a gringo serial killer. Federales say it's a foreigner, or a gang of foreigners. Bus drivers. An Egyptian. Street gangs. Narco smugglers. Americans say it's the Mexican cops themselves. The year 2003 brought the hideous allegation that the women were actually being harvested by a shadowy syndicate of transplant-organ providers. It sounded like a story from a book of urban myths or a bad horror movie: young women cut up and sold, liver by liver, heart by heart, to wealthy white folks, and while the harvesters are doing their butchering, they stop for a bit of rape and torture to make it interesting.

Susana Flores, a thirteen-year-old girl, was mercifully shot in the head. After all, the coroner discovered that during her torture, she had suffered four heart attacks. Imagine her pleading, her tears. Imagine what made a young girl suffer heart attack after heart attack after heart attack after heart attack before the Angel of Sorrow laid a tender gun to her skull and pulled the trigger. Even on the border, there is sometimes grace.

Steve Ganitsch, the uber-officer of the Cactus Cops, says: "Five miles from the border, nobody knows. Nobody cares. Nobody understands. They don't want to know."

|||||||

In Organ Pipe, ranger Chris Eggle, everyone's all-American, your favorite daydream of what a ranger would be—an Eagle Scout, a class president from Michigan, a tall clear-eyed handsome man that fellow officers said was the embodiment of the Spirit of Christmas—was gunned down by two scuttling hitmen from Tijuana. How like Desolation to surprise Chris Eggle with a burst of gunfire on a bright beautiful day with the heat roaring up out of the land and the hard disk of blue scraping overhead. The gunmen had tied up their victims outside of Sonoita. Drugs. Fifteen thousand dollars a head. They shot each man in the back, full auto, rattatatta squirming and jerking in the dirt. Federales got on to them—the desert dropped a dime somehow and the cops came swarming, more blood, more blood—and the Tijuana *sicarios* fled down to the tourist area near the Gulf of California, totally screwed here in Sonora, no paid-off cops anywhere, no narco bigwigs to protect them: the only narcos for three hundred miles would torture them for days before tossing them into the Pinacate to be eaten piecemeal by coyotes and crows. But they were also totally tweaked on the buzz, the outlaw scramble. Loud music. Gunsmoke. They carjacked an SUV and tore into the Devil's Highway, jumping the border and thinking they were clear of the Mexican cavalry. But the Federales jumped the line, too, undocumented entrants, all right, bristling with M16s and chrome magnums. As the SUV skidded into Organ Pipe and Chris Eggle got out of his vehicle, perhaps wondering what would happen, wondering how to reason with these boys, a helicopter overhead watching it all, when the drug killer leaped out, all desperado, all fired up, all panicky, jazzed beyond belief with the chase and the stench of the assassination blood all over his feet, and he blasted Chris Eggle.

Eggle's Kevlar vest could handle most rounds, but the one that went low bounced off his holstered weapon and took a ninety-degree detour under his vest and tore into his middle. The gunman must have thought he'd won the lottery; he turned to flee toward the Mexican line, perhaps thinking it all seemed like a good idea at the time, maybe thinking of home, of his lover, of shelter at the last second, when the Federales said "Hi there." Thirty illegal Mexican cops appeared in the brush and opened up on him. It was a scene from a Clint Eastwood movie, a hellstorm of bullets.

One of the agents complained that only one of the Federales managed to hit him.

"What's wrong with those people?" he said. "Thirty guys opening up and nobody hits him. No wonder they're in trouble."

The Mexicans were warmly invited to recross their border and go home. The perpetrator died, "Crying like a baby and squealing like a pig." Observers watched the Mexican bellow and sob. They might not have rushed him to a hospital.

A border cop confessed: "I have a rule now. If it don't speak English, shoot it."

| | | | | | | |

Summer 2002: a coffin-load was crammed into the trunk of a Mazda south of Tucson. Riders also filled the seats in the car. The Coyote sped into town and was immediately targeted by the local police. A wild chase ensued, with the driver leading Tucson cops in and out of the outskirts, banging over railroad tracks and sliding in the sand that flows onto the streets like water. The driver got to the edge of town and bailed out. All his riders jumped out and vanished into the desert. Except for the two men in the trunk.

Department of Public Safety officer Robert Telles inspected the car. There were no regulations stating that he had to jimmy the trunk open. Perhaps only a Border Patrol agent would have the kind of dark imagination to know there might be humans locked inside. Officer Telles followed procedure and slapped a yellow tow-away sticker on the windshield. Impounded.

The tow crew was slow to get out there, however. The car sat beside the road for two days. Temperatures soared well over the hundred mark. When the tow truck finally arrived, the crew noted the stench. They pried the trunk open. Two young men lay within. They were twenty-one and sixteen years old. The police reported there was evidence of "movement" in the trunk before the two young men baked to death.

Movement.

And God continued to flog his children with unusual fury. In the eastern desert of Arizona, a group of entrants was struck by lightning. Bound bodies, supposedly of Mexicans, began to appear in the brush. They had been laid facedown, with their hands tied behind them, and shot in the heads. Various theories attribute the crime to vigilante Aryan "citizens' border patrols" freelancing the chaos along the line, or to rival Coyote mobs exterminating walkers to make a point; paranoiac border watchers imagine a rogue Border Patrol death squad. In Texas, two FBI agents investigating Mexican train robbers who jumped freight trains near the El Paso line were mobbed by a gang of Mexicans and dragged to the border, where they were savagely beaten. One of them died. In Iowa, a train car was famously pried open to reveal the cooked and melted remains of eleven entrants. The world's biggest coffin-load. A Mexican drowned on live television trying to swim across the pathetically narrow Rio Grande. He looked almost funny. He belly flopped into the water, splashed, splashed—it couldn't have been more than two, three strokes— and he was gone. Just . . . gone. They played it as a tape loop: splash-splash-gone; splash-splash-gone.

The Yuma 14 changed nothing, and they changed everything.

|||||||

Today, Mendez sits in a cell in the big prison in Safford, Arizona. He has no visitors. He doesn't answer letters.

The spirits of the dead moved the living in Desolation to make changes. Some of the changes are symbolic, too little, too late. The Mexicans opened a small consulate in Yuma, though the consuls agree that the Yuma consulate is an empty gesture. Tucson, yes. Calexico, yes. Phoenix, yes. But Yuma . . . well. It's a building with a Mexican flag, and it balances out the Border Patrol offices out on the east end of town. The power remains in Calexico; the main consulate is still in Phoenix. Nobody goes to Yuma.

Yuma sector faced strange changes after the event. Mike F., the signcutter who happened along the Vidrios Drag that first morning, went over to the K9 corps. Yuma Migra agents close ranks around him when asked if he's available for an interview. "Sorry," you're told. "He's with the canine units now. He can't be bothered." They don't think you should use his name. Other aspects of the Yuma 14 case—BORTAC operations, for example, investigative leads—are under OP/SEC secret clearance, need-to-know, eyes only. Makes everybody feel like they're James Bond.

One thing Yuma and Wellton understood immediately from the disaster in May was that the way things worked didn't work. If they were to hope for a change in the fate of the Devil's Highway and all the lost souls walking it, they would have to become proactive, not reactive. They arrested plenty of walkers, but they wanted to save more of them. This quiet resolve is reflected in the way they refer to the catastrophe in obtuse terms— not "Yuma 14" for them. They still say "The thing that happened" when they speak of it. As if it were too sad to name.

One of the first things Yuma did was to organize a crack BORSTAR unit. They immediately began to patrol by helicopter, four-by truck, and ATV. Sometimes, the helicopter ferried the agents and their small all-terrain scooters in by air, and they dropped into the danger zone and sped to the rescue. Each member of the unit spoke fluent Spanish, had been through a demanding boot camp experience, was trained in emergency medicine. Most BORSTAR agents were military men, like Yuma's Jason Carroll, a former sniper.

││││││││

In Wellton, things were even more immediate. After all, it was in their patrol area that the deaths happened, and it was their guys who had first rushed to save the walkers. In a stroke of genius, Wellton trucked in portable army buildings and dropped them right in the middle of the Devil's Highway, beside the Pinacate Lava Flow. The units were plain cubes, with room extenders that slid out on the sides. Water buffalo trucks set up huge water tanks outside. Radio antennae and satellite dishes went on top, generators roared to life, and small groups of agents took up permanent residence in the heart of the walking zone. It was a substation in the wilderness. Patrols had a base in the very middle of the traffic, and patrols could go out all night; the lights of the camp were visible to walkers for miles.

Not satisfied with the substation, Wellton's agents invented another, more extreme bit of ingenuity. It was obvious that the main corridor north tended to be in the deadly area of the bombing range, hemmed in on either side by the ABC mountains and the Gilas. Sooner or later, most walkers entered that vast alley and headed for the freeway.

Agent John Bergkretter designed a lifesaving tower. It was an engineering marvel. Thirty feet tall, with a crown of aluminum reflectors hanging like fishing lures and flashing in the sun, each tower has a beacon that flashes every ten seconds. Visible day and night. Each tower is powered by a solar panel and a battery. On the pole, there are signs with illustrations, in Spanish and English.

Like Nahum Landa's testimony, it's a kind of found poetry:

ATTENTION!
You cannot walk to safety from
this point! You are in danger
of Dying if you do not
summon help!

If you need help,
Push red button.
US Border Patrol
Will arrive in 1 Hour.

Do Not Leave This Location!

The towers are raised in such a fashion that walkers can see them from a distance, and each leads to the next. Ultimately, the towers will lead from Mexico to the I-8 corridor.

Each tower costs six thousand dollars.

Environmentalists tried to stop them: towers would ruin the landscape. Critics railed against the towers, like they criticized the Samaritan groups out rescuing walkers, or the humanitarian outfits placing bottled water and canned food in marked locations for them, and still, conservative pundits try to get their constituents to believe the American Taxpayer, that mythical and handy beast, is funding lifesaving towers foisted on them by the lily-livered INS, which, by the way, allowed hijackers to blow up New York. Instead of closed and secure borders, "orange freeway cones," comfort stations, and expensive light towers.

Wrong.

In fact, the towers are built, raised, maintained, and paid for out-of-pocket by those bleeding-heart liberals, the Border Patrol agents themselves.

In Arizona, critics are more direct. Immigration protests have a homegrown cowboy feel to them. Toxic materials appear in jugs that look like drinking water. Humane Borders' water stations are vandalized, the three-hundred-gallon tanks broken open so they run dry. Small groups of Mexicans are found tied and shot in the head.

The Border Patrol is sentimental, though, and they keep building towers.

On June 14, 2002, the beacons got their first test. A group of three walkers was overwhelmed by the 107-degree heat. At 9:48 in the morning, they hit the panic button. Old boys from Wellton were on the road in seconds. They were at the tower in twenty-four minutes. Like the Wellton 26, these walkers had left a group behind—seventeen more walkers were tracked and bagged by the cutters. It took one hour from button-push to rescue.

In the year after the Wellton 26 lost their way, Tucson sector racked up deaths in the hundreds. Yuma sector managed to reduce the season's death rate to nine.

||||||||

Consul Flores Vizcarra says it isn't the desert that kills immigrants. It isn't Coyotes. It isn't even the Border Patrol.

"What kills the people," he says, "is the politics of stupidity that rules both sides of the border."

Firebrand lawyer and human rights activist Isabel García is the spokeswoman for Derechos Humanos, and cochair of the Arizona Border Rights Project. She is seen as a beacon in her own right. She has battled the Migra for long hard years. Towers? The Border Patrol's lifesaving tactics are "like throwing a child in the ocean and then throwing in floaties afterward. It's not sufficient, and we think it's disingenuous to say they're making it safer. Our border policies are the direct cause of those fourteen deaths."

And, "For the U.S. to attempt to put all of the blame for these deaths on one individual or two individuals or three individuals really sidesteps their responsibility in this."

Mendez could have used her on his team.

During this whole event, the rescue, the trials and the aftermath, an average of one person a day died somewhere on the border, trying to get those last few miles toward the big American lights.

||||||||

Perhaps, ultimately, what is so remarkable about the Mexican border is not how many of Them have come across, but how many of Them have not. It is not hard to imagine any one of the Wellton 26 deciding it was time to put a roof on the house, to build a small concrete room for the new baby, to buy furniture for his wife, to feed his family. Their reasons for coming were as simple as that—as were the reasons Mendez says he came. It is important to remember that Mendez himself never intended to be a Coyote—he was settling in on the Mexican side of the border. To hear politicians and talk show hosts tell it, the entire population of Mexico is on its way. We try to put numbers on a story that is, at base, a story of the heart.

Numbers never lie, after all: they simply tell different stories depending on the math of the tellers.

The same facts and figures add up to different sums. The Center for Immigration Studies did a number crunch in 2001, and they came up with the alarming data that each illegal costs the United States money. "The estimated lifetime net fiscal drain (taxes paid minus services used) for the average adult Mexican immigrant is negative $55,200." That is, welfare, medical services, school services, various outreaches, cost us $55K+ over a lifetime of menial labor. The Mexican Migration Project (MMP) points out that harsher border policies, including the famous Operation Gatekeeper and its ilk, ensure that illegal immigrants stay for long periods—thus ensuring some percentage of that $55K+ prophecy comes to fruition.

Several studies have also pointed out that illegal immigrants actually depress wages. They help keep the minimum wage down. This means savings for the managers: Captains of Industry and loyal Dittoheads in the grand cirque du capitalisme are saving money on low wages and cheaper product. That can of peas we eat doesn't cost $9.98, not until the Wobblies get in there and organize a real union. Vicks VapoRub is bottled in Mexico; Big Macs are cooked by Mexicans. Shaving points off both ends.

Although the federal tax figure is decried in some of the reports as minimal—after all, these are poor folks who make $4.50 an hour—it is still worth considering. If there are eight million tonks slaving away in the United States right now (and one of the Mexican pols interviewed for this book crowed, "We have inserted twelve million workers into the United States—it is already Mexico! We have won the war!"), most of those workers pay federal income tax: shaved right off the top. No choice, just like you. They pay state taxes: shaved right off the top. They get tapped for Social Security and FICA. There's a whole lot of shaving going on. If you multiply $4.50 an hour by eight million workers, that would mean there are thirty-six million taxable dollars being accrued every hour by illegals getting tapped for some percentage by Uncle Sam. Those workers will not receive a refund. State tax? Has the governor of California gotten a new swimming pool lately? How's the governor's mansion in Baton Rouge looking?

Lower wages, cheaper product, unclaimed federal taxes, unclaimed state taxes, unused Social Security. Over a lifetime, does it start to ameliorate the $55K+? What about sales taxes, gas tax, rent? What about Pampers at the local Vons supermarket? Cigarette tax. Beer. Tortillas and BVDs and cable and used cars and speeding tickets and water bills and electric bills and tampons and Trojans and Mars bars. Movie tickets. Running shoes. CDs. Over a lifetime, how much does it add to the American commonwealth?

But they take away our jobs! Interestingly, the U.S. Bureau of Labor Satistics has reported that by 2008, there will be five million more jobs in the United States than people to do them. This is after the tides of illegals. After the post-Iraq economic doldrums. Even if we vacuum up the homeless and set them to sweeping and frying, we'll have a few million vacancies. Who you gonna call?

UCLA's North American Integration and Development Center (you can hear talk radio hosts protesting already— UCLA! Commie bastards!) released a twenty-first-century study that found that "undocumented immigrants" contributed "at least $300 billion per year to the U.S. gross domestic product (GDP)." If you put their numbers at a mere 4.5 million, they still add between $154 million and $220 billion, the report says. Researcher Marisol Sanchez told the EFE News Service, apropos of this study, that "although conservative groups claim that undocumented immigrants are a social burden," illegals tend to shy away from seeking social services because they don't want to be deported. Wherefore $55K+?

How many toys. How many phone bills. How much in the poor box at church. How much for pencils, steaks, charcoal, glasses, panties, bras, bikes, skateboards, concerts, Blockbuster, Monistat, Head & Shoulders, Listerine. AOL. Computers. Backpacks. Uniforms. Night school.

What of the Devil's Highway itself, the tormented border in Arizona?

In June 2003, right in the heart and heat of the killing season, Thunderbird, the American Graduate School of International Management, released a study. Sooner or later, everyone will release a study. But this one made the Mexican consuls of Arizona happy. No doubt Vicente Fox faxed it to the White House.

Thunderbird learned that Arizona "gets $8 billion in economic impact annually from the relationship" with Mexico. That's profit, not costs. Mexico makes $5.5 billion. Reymundo and his son would have been stunned to know they were dying under a high tide of money. Critics will be stunned to learn that the United States makes more money in the deal than those wily Mexicans.

Thunderbird relates:

"Mexican immigrants paid nearly $600 million in federal taxes and sales taxes in 2002 . . . Mexican immigrants use about $250 million in social services such as Medicaid and food stamps . . . Another $31 million in uncompensated health care. . . ."

That leaves a profit of $319 million.

The Arizona Republic further quotes the report:

- The average annual wage for Arizonans is $28,355; for the state's Mexican immigrants it's $12,963.
- The total buying power of Arizona's Mexican immigrants is estimated at $4.18 billion.
- The state's Mexican immigrants spend an estimated $1.5 billion in mortgage payments and rent annually.
- Mexican tourists and visitors spent $962 million in Arizona in 2001, while state residents spent about $328 million in Mexico.
- Remittances from the state's Mexican immigrants to their homeland reached $486 million last year, with those trans-

actions generating about $57 million in fees to Arizona banks and financial institutions.

We not only gonna get it back, but we gonna pay for it, too . . .

| | | | | | | |

The investigation over, the afternoon growing late, the light fades in the Tucson consulate's office. The scented candles are guttering low now, but they still give up their scent. The death pictures of the Yuma 14 go back in their envelopes, to be filed and forgotten. Their bodies are long gone, gone and buried. Still, the smell of death floats in the room as the tainted papers and cardboard folders are sealed. It's dark and leathery, smells like burned barbecue and old trash, at once tangy and flat.

A woman in stretch pants sits across the room. She has scuffed white shoes and holds a cracking vinyl purse with a faux-gold clasp in her lap. She wrings its tan shoulder straps in her fists. She's sitting on the edge of the seat, and she has pins in her hair, and she is smiling and bowing her head, enacting the ancient pantomime of subservience that Mexicans of humble origin rely on to help them deal with people of power. Like consulate secretaries sitting behind big desks.

She has come to ask the secretary about a certain Juan García who walked into the Sonora desert a week ago and never came out in Arizona.

The security chief is saying, "They drink piss to live!"

"Excuse me, sir," the secretary says.

"What is it?"

"This señora has lost a Juan García."

"How long?"

"A week or more," the woman offers.

"Oh, yeah. We've got him."

She smiles.

"Yes?" she says.

"He's dead. I've got him on the slab."

The chief walks out. The secretary walks out.

The woman sits alone, staring at the desk. She looks up. "What do I do now?" she asks.

I I I I I I I I

Just as the last file is going to go on the shelf, a coroner's report slides out. It's Reymundo Sr.'s death certificate. Compared to his son's, it's almost an exact replica. Before the files are sealed and stowed away, to be unread forever, the Yuma 14 have one final surprise to offer. File after file says the same thing. Reymundo, and his son, all of them, have been listed in death as WHITE MALE.

The secretary comes back in and notes the woman is crying.

"Oh!" she says. "We've upset you." She sits and says, "Señora, you must forgive us. We deal with death so often in here that we forget. We forget, you see. We're indelicate. If you don't work here, death still means something to you."

She smiles as she collects the files. The chief comes back in and takes the grieving woman by the arm.

"Let's get your man," he says.

The files go on the shelf; a stack of newer files is dislodged and falls over. It is almost dark now. The secretary pats her hair into place, then bends once at each desk, and with a small puff from her deep red lips, blows out the candles.

ACKNOWLEDGMENTS

| | | | | | | | |

I owe thanks to many. Their generosity and expertise made this complex investigation possible. Most assuredly, any errors are my own.

Any writer undertaking a project such as this can only hope for a veteran investigative journalist for a partner. My wife, Cinderella, did more than her share of work. She set up a database, ran the computer, surfed the AP newswires and the LexisNexis cyberservice. She arranged interviews, worked the phones, and accompanied me to some of the meetings. She occasionally wrangled with the Border Patrol. Finally, she was my first reader and my first editor, keeping my nose to the news and my head out of the stars.

Tucson author, and my legal counsel, Brian Andrew Laird Esq. took part in many uncomfortable adventures as I sniffed around. Bad miles, the smell of death, many hot roads, cheap motel rooms, bad stares from Migra agents. Laird broke a few laws in our first uninvited penetration of the Goldwater range, nearly broke his axles in jaunts across forbidden landscapes. He sat with me as we peeled open the death packets in the Tucson consulate. And later, he survived our car wreck with armed Chicano drug mules on the rez. Viva Pelón.

IIIIIIII

I am indebted to the Mexican consular corps for generous help and support at every turn. Late in the game, San Diego consul Felipe Cuellar and his wife, Calexico consul Rita Vargas, were stationed in Chicago. Rita, as the manuscript reveals, happened to be the Mexican official in charge of the entire "Yuma 14" investigation. She and Felipe proofread my manuscript and caught me out in foolish errors. They hosted me to long locked-door meetings at the Chicago consulate. And Rita made her diaries of the event available to me. I will forever be in their debt.

My cousin, Enrique Hubbard Urrea, is the Mexican ambassador to the Philippines. Even from that great distance, his presence and name opened doors for me. His books lent a welcome bit of clarity to my understanding of Mexican politics. I'm waiting for him to become president.

His son, Alan Hubbard, in the security wing of the Phoenix consulate, made many incredibly valuable documents available to me, as well as the addresses and phone numbers of the survivors, and many notes on the structure of the Cercas gang's Coyote empire. In Tucson, consul Carlos Flores Vizcarra was generous with his time and wisdom. He opened his archives to us and allowed us to inspect them and observe the daily operations of the consulate. His public affairs agent, Dulce, was professional and kind, and I am grateful to her for helping us penetrate their secretive world.

Finally, in Mexico City, a spirit hovering over much of this investigation is Gustavo Mohar, cacique of the consular corps.

In Phoenix, Mendez's federal defender, Gerald Williams, gave us hours of his time. He turned over reams of information, and stacks of invaluable tapes. He also delivered messages to Mendez.

| | | | | | | | |

This book would be nowhere, however, without La Pinche Migra. For some reason, the Border Patrol decided to take a risk and, after long and fruitless courting, allowed me to enter the back rooms and the trucks. They were both open and guarded. But they were honest, even when it was not in their best interest. They showed me how to cut sign, and they stood on the Devil's Highway with me and looked into Mexico with a certain sense of regret and unexpected compassion. Several of the agents have kept me updated via e-mail and telephone on developments in their personal and professional lives.

Wellton's supervisory agent, Kenneth Smith, a thirty-year veteran, was my Yoda as I tried to penetrate their world. I think of the hours we spent with gratitude. Ken was a boon companion, and he helped put a human face on the Border Patrol.

Agent Jerome Wofford worked the computers and showed me the death scene photos and analyzed what the death-sign meant. Yuma's Mike McGlasson was the exemplary information officer and good Marine. He opened the doors for me. I wouldn't want to be a Coyote with Mike on my trail. Mike's harem of newswomen was also a delight to work with. Officer Friendly gave me a bunch of shit, and it was a great help in getting the feel of the station. He suggests that the proper title for this book is *Coyote Bait*. Miss Anne, in Wellton Station, was kind.

I must thank Jason Carroll, of BORSTAR, for excellent informative sessions. By phone and e-mail, Jason helped me decipher arcana—including the finer points of drinking urine. Tucson sector was tougher to enter than Yuma. Agent Ryan Scudder is greatly admired by the Mexican consuls, and he was helpful. Information officer Rob Daniels was informative. And in Washington, D.C., Mario Villareal was the master of the brush-out.

Former BP agent Warrior offered generous thoughts and prayers late in the game.

The Border Patrol's PowerPoint presentation of "Operation Broken Promise" was a valuable tool.

King of the Cactus Cops, Steve Ganitsch, was a great blessing. There were moments when other law enforcement agents were so astounded that Ganitsch was my friend that they gave up secrets immediately.

||||||||

Chuck Bowden, as always, was helpful and generous; a boon companion and a walking encyclopedia of border and desert lore.

Rick Ufford-Chase and the Samaritan Patrols based in Tucson were extremely helpful and open. I learned much from them, and I admire their example.

Dr. Ralph Cintron, at University of Illinois at Chicago, sent me valuable research materials. César A. González, at San Diego Mesa College, was as always a mentor and provider of valuable articles and insights. At UIC, graduate student JoAnne Ruvoli-Gruba provided me with materials about BORSTAR and some Border Patrol history. San Diego PD's Great Dispatcher, Kyle Wiggins, helped out. Natalie Sudman introduced me to the Cactus Cop, and without her intervention, all the subsequent doors might not have opened. Thanks to my colleagues on the advisory board of the Paso Al Norte Immigration Museum of El Paso, Texas.

Tony Delcavo, of Bella Luna Books, caught my single greatest typo: I apparently uncovered a "vast conspiracy of snuggling." It would be a different border if that were true.

Stewart O'Nan, as always, was the world's best sounding board: his insights into narrative choices and editing were invaluable.

My unbelievable editor, Geoff Shandler, found the heart of this book. And everyone at the Dijkstra Agency makes it possible for me to go into battle.

Thanks to Rich Hopkins and the mighty Sidewinders.

Finally, thanks to the members of the band Calexico—their song "Across the Wire" appeared unexpectedly and lent moral support when it was deeply needed.

| | | | | | | |

The news publications accessed in this project were: The *Arizona Daily Star*, the *Arizona Republic*, the *Chicago Tribune*, the *Denver Post*, the *El Paso Times*, *Global News Wire/EFE News Service*, *La Jornada*, the *Los Angeles Times*, the *New York Times*, *Newsday*, *La Opinión*, *Outside* magazine, *Range* magazine, Salon.com, the *San Diego Reader*, the *San Diego Union Tribune*, the *Tucson Citizen*, the *Tucson Weekly*, the *Wall Street Journal*, the *Washington Post*, *Zeta*. Ray Rojas's Internet news service out of Texas was always a welcome source of information: Ray is the Xicano Drudge Report—even has a cool fedora. Of all the papers covering the border, the *Daily Star* of Arizona and the *Arizona Republic* are the invaluable sources, and the *Star's* Web site offers a constant stream of illuminating border stories. For portraits of the Veracruz home and the relatives of the Yuma 14, the *Tucson Citizen* is of interest. Border Patrol Web sites and officer's union Web sites were also of great interest. Mike McGlasson provided me with a healthy flow of Yuma sector press releases. The Samaritans e-mailed me their minutes after every meeting. And, of course, the aforementioned AP and LexisNexis services. My maps were U.S. Geological Survey topo maps that divided up the entire region into detailed sections. For a quick overview of the state of Arizona, the *Arizona Atlas and Gazetteer* from DeLorme Mapping was extremely handy. If anyone wishes to learn about the Devil's Highway region, they need only step into Tucson's Map and Flag Center, where Mr. F. Keith Trantow and the staff will orient and guide with a sure hand.

Thanks to P. K. Weis of the *Citizen* for his excellent photographs.

Several reports and monographs, from both the Right and the Left, were eye-opening. One of the most interesting was the Population Council's December 1, 2001, report, "Death at the Border: Efficacy and Unintended Consequences of U.S. Immigration Control Policy," by Wayne A. Cornelius. Another was the Center for Immigration Studies Forum press conference from the Nixon Center in Washington, D.C., in August 2002. (Transcript available from the Federal News Service.) The Border Information Outreach Service can be accessed via *www.us-mex.org/borderlines*. The Mexican Migration Project (MMP) has done some interesting research into the issue. An outgrowth of this research is the valuable book *Beyond Smoke and Mirrors: Mexican Immigration in an Era of Economic Integration*, by Massey, Durand, and Malone.

For those who want to keep an eye on the Mexicans, there are three excellent Web sites that pull back the tortilla curtain and make secrets visible. They are invaluable for anyone seeking to do thorough homework. These are: El Colegio de la Frontera Norte, *www.colef.mx*; Instituto Nacional de Estadistica, Geografía e Información, *www.inegi.mx*; and Consejo Nacional de Población, *www.conapo.mx*.

For a liberal/humanitarian angle on the border, interested readers should look into Humane Borders and Derechos Humanos and the American Friends Service Committee.

Anyone seeking a deeper understanding of the border might want to read the excellent anthologies put out by Cinco Puntos Press, in El Paso. Both *The Late Great Mexican Border* and *Puro Border* offer insights into the world of the Coyotes and the rich and troubled border world. The latter has an invaluable dictionary/lexicon of Coyote and pollo slang.

Certainly, anyone looking into the Devil's Highway region must begin with John Annerino's text, *Dead in Their Tracks*. Perhaps the earliest book about the Devil's Highway region, barring the conquistadors' chronicles, is Nils and Dorothy Hogner's *Westward Ho! High, Low and Dry*. If you find a copy, let me know.

Charles Bowden's books are an invaluable source of border/desert information; of particular value to the writing of this book were *Blue Desert* and *Desierto*. Both Bowden and Annerino feature versions of the Melchior Díaz story. Rubén Martinez has written a classic of border literature, *Crossing Over*. Anyone who wants to understand the world of the undocumented entrant could do worse than to start here. For the bad-Mexicans and evil-Arabs crowd, Michelle Malkin's alarmist screed *Invasion* is satisfyingly hair-raising.

Aron Spilken's *Escape!* is a study of a similar tragedy to the one described in this book; it took place in the same general area. For some sense of the awfulness of the Devil's Highway region in cowboy days, readers are wise to read the last half of Cormac McCarthy's apocalyptic historical novel, *Blood Meridian*. Many other border/desert writers are worth looking into. Writers whose work also affected this book: John Alcock, Craig Childs, James W. Clarke, Ted Conover, Bernard Fontana, Julian Hayden, Gary Paul Nabhan, Sam Quinones, Sebastian Rotella— particularly his excellent *Twilight on the Line: Underworlds and Politics at the Mexican Border*.

INDEX

| | | | | | | |

Maradona, Rodrigo, 68, 73–74, 80–81,
  83
  as *guía*, 88–90, 105, 108, 117, 194,
    203
  in Sonoita, 84, 99–100
"Marias," 39, 84
Marin, Claudio Alejandro (Yuma
  14/Wellton 26), 147, 174, 192
Marines, 26, 79, 133, 172, 174, 184, 186
Martinez, Edgar (Yuma 14/Wellton
  26), 146, 163–65, 175–76, 193
Martinez, Eugenio, 164
Martinez de la Torre (Mexico), 144
Matamoros (Mexico), 206
materias (mediums), 87
Maya Indians, 48, 147
Mendez (Yuma 14/Wellton 26)
  background of, 70, 73–74, 189
  capture of, 90–91
  confession of, 68, 70, 188–90,
    194–95, 215
  defense of, 199–200, 215
  in Guadalajara, 67, 73–74, 99, 199,
    202
  haircut of (Rooster Boy), 67, 72, 75,
    100, 102, 185–86
  in jail, 199, 211
  with Lauro, 157–61, 165, 169–72
  in Nogales, 70, 73–75, 100, 189
  recruitment of, 70, 73–78
  rescue of, 174–75, 181, 189, 191
  in Sonoita, 67, 83–102
  veering of, 112–13, 135, 138–39
  with Yuma 14/Wellton 26, 102–17,
    134–42, 145, 149–57
  See also Lopez Ramos, Jesús Antonio
Mendez, Celia Lomas, 67, 88, 98, 100,
  194–95, 200, 203
mestizos, 11, 39, 44, 51, 122
Mexicali (Mexico), 182–83, 206
Mexican consulate. *See* consulates,
  Mexican
Mexican Migration Project, 216
Mexico
  army of, 55, 80, 195
  economic policies of, 44–45, 134,
    145, 204–6
  history of, 8–10, 77
  illegals policy and, 54–56, 76–77
  immigration police of, 95, 133
  as oppressor, 75–76, 134
  Spanish conquest of, 9–10, 43, 48
Mexico City (Mexico)

bus from, 91, 94, 147
life in, 182, 197
siting of, 9, 43–44, 77, 93
La Migra
  BORTAC SWAT troops of, 79, 89,
    201–2, 212
  as enemy, 74–76, 78, 82, 107–11, 134,
    146, 200
  and Operation Gatekeeper, 18–19,
    58–59, 91, 216
  as rescuers, 124, 140, 150, 162,
    170–72, 189
  See also Border Patrol
mile marker 27, 13, 63–64, 109
militias, civilian, 8, 79–80, 110
missionaries, 7, 9, 11, 34, 44, 88
Mixtec Indians, 39
Mohawk Mountains, 80, 156, 169
Mohawk rest area, 7, 64, 81, 160,
  169–70, 191
Mohawk Valley, 20, 172, 191
money
  as bribes, 44, 55, 81, 83, 97, 102
  to bus drivers, 81, 83, 97, 102
  Coyote costs, 34, 49–50, 60–63,
    69–70, 180
  for death details, 37–38, 196, 199
  to *guía*, 66–67, 69–70, 74
  as loans, 49–50, 144–45, 147
  to Mendez, 151–56, 201
  as remittance from U.S., 45–46,
    218–19
  for safe house, 89, 97
Monreal Well, 139
Morales Hernandez, Abraham (Yuma
  14/Wellton 26), 105, 163–64, 174,
  193
Morales Jimenez, Francisco (Yuma
  14/Wellton 26)
  account of, 152–53, 162, 164–65
mordidas (bribes), 44
El Moreno, 62, 65, 104
motels/hotels, 55, 80–81, 84–85, 88–89,
  91, 97, 149
Mount Ajo, 85
Mounted Chinese Exclusionary Police,
  8
La Mujer Azul, 11
mules (human), 15, 39
Municipio de Huellapan (Mexico), 139
Muñoz, Nelly, 89, 92, 97, 100, 102, 147
music
  banda style, 73, 75–76, 98, 202

Puerto Blanco Mountains, 85–86
Puerto Peñasco, 87

Quelele (the Carrion Hawk), 12
Quitobaquito Hills, 57, 89

railroads, 7–8, 20, 39, 204, 211
Raven's Butte, 5, 26, 172
recruitment
  in barrio, 62
  of González brothers, 91
  of Mendez, 70, 73–78
  of Yuma 14/Wellton 26, 48–52,
    92–96, 134, 144–45, 184, 196
  See also García, Don Moises
Red Tanks Wells, 86
revolutionaries, 76–77, 94
Reyes, Claudia, 146, 164
Río Grande (El Río Bravo), 96, 211
Rocky Mountains, 116
Rocky Point, 87
Rodriguez, José de Jesús (Yuma
    14/Wellton 26), 143, 159, 165
Romo, Toribio, 78
Rooster Cogburn Ostrich Ranch,
    119–20, 192
Route 2 (Mexico), 20, 80–81, 83, 87, 89

safe houses, 62, 65, 89, 92, 97, 100–102,
    147, 149
Safford (Arizona), 211
saguaro cactus
  as desert fixture, 4, 14–15, 27–28, 57,
    83, 105, 200
  as signpost, 26, 29
  spines of, 5–6, 83, 105
Salazar, Francisco, 12
Salvadorans, 18, 44
Samaritans, 214
San Antonio Hotel (Sonoita). *See* Hotel
    San Antonio
Sanchez, Marisol, 217
San Diego (California)
  border crossing in, 18–19, 58, 60, 91,
    179
  Mexican consulate in, 182
Sand Papagos Indians. *See* Papago
    Indians
Sand Tank Mountains, 78
San Luis (Arizona), 18, 55, 81
San Luis Potosí (Mexico), 94
San Luis Río Colorado (Mexico), 75,
    80, 83, 85, 91, 103, 182

San Pedro Altepepan (Mexico), 143
Santa Fe (New Mexico), 58
Santería, 88
Santillan, Javier (Yuma 14/Wellton 26),
    147
Santos (Yuma 14/Wellton 26)
  disappearance of, 140–41, 200
  with Mendez, 105, 107, 135, 137–38,
    200
  as *pollero*, 85, 89, 100–101, 104
San Ysidro (Arizona), 59
Sasabe (Mexico), 19, 55–56, 58–60, 83
Satanists, 207
Scala, Lisa, 118
Scarface Mountain, 85–86
Scudder, Ryan (agent), 54
segundas (flea markets), 46, 207
Sells (Arizona), 7, 13, 63
Shadow Wolves, 79
Sheep Mountain, 81
sheriffs, 7, 35, 71–72, 133, 148, 173,
    182, 184
Sierra Madre Occidental, 94
Sierra Madre Oriental, 44
Sierra Madre del Sur, 44
Sierra Pinta, 156
Sierrita Mountains, 55
signcutters (trackers)
  among Coyotes, 28–30, 63, 86, 90
  of Border Patrol, 7, 17, 28–31, 109,
    128, 171, 174, 205
  and bug-sign, 30, 116
  of Wellton station, 26, 67, 201, 214
  and Yuma 14/Wellton 26, 111–13,
    133–34, 138–39, 159, 166, 196
Smith, Kenny (agent), 21–22, 30–31, 54,
    67, 167, 172
smuggling
  of drugs, 15, 31, 79
  of illegals, 13, 34, 54, 57, 78, 189, 202
  See also Coyotes; narcotics trade
El Sol del Desierto (Sonoita), 89
Sonoita (Mexico), 9, 187, 208
  as border crossing, 84–97
  Coyote operations in, 47, 55, 62–63,
    72, 81, 194, 206
  Mendez in, 67, 83–102
  Yuma 14/Wellton 26 in, 58, 97, 100,
    145, 147, 149
Sonora (Mexico), 8, 47, 55, 58, 62–63,
    197
  See also Altar; Nogales; San Luis Río
    Colorado; Sonoita

Sonoran Desert
   animals of, 5–6, 94, 117, 134, 200
   birds of, 115–18, 136
   creosote bush in, 14, 29, 57, 90, 105,
      137, 157
   heat of, 5, 14, 25, 115–29, 137–38,
      147, 152, 164, 174, 188–89, 210,
      214
   insects of, 6, 19, 30, 57, 115–17, 147,
      192
   ironwood trees in, 4, 12, 27
   mesquite trees in, 4, 6, 90, 117, 137,
      157, 162
   mountains of, 85–86, 117, 119, 156,
      172, 192
   paloverde trees in, 14, 90, 104, 117
   snakes of, 6, 26–27, 117
   water sources in, 7, 12, 86, 134, 139
Sonoyta. *See* Sonoita
Sonoyta Arroyo, 87
Sonoyta Mountains, 85
Spains Well, 139
"Stolen at Gunpoint" (song), 76
Surem (spirit), 6
survivors
   in hospital, 71–72, 181–82, 185
   on Mendez, 67, 107, 145, 152–57,
      185–86
   narratives of, 104–9, 133–37, 148–68,
      186–87, 201, 203
   See also Yuma 14/Wellton 26: rescue
      of

Tabasco (Mexico), 43
Tacna (Arizona), 85
tanks, abandoned, 5, 26
Taoists, 87
Tapia, Heriberto (Yuma 14/Wellton
   26), 147
Telles, Robert (officer), 210
Temich González, Rafael (Yuma
   14/Wellton 26), 138, 147–48
   account of, 141, 152, 154–56, 158, 167
   in hospital, 181–82, 185
Temporal Pass, 136, 138
Teresa (Cercas gang), 63–64
terrorists, 15, 39, 204–5
Texas Rangers, 17
Thunderbird. *See* American Graduate
   School of International
   Management
Tijuana (Mexico), 8, 73, 91, 96, 182,
   206, 208

Tijuana No (rock band), 76
Tijuana River, 59
tinajas (water holes), 7, 86
Tinajas Altas Mountains, 25, 56, 67, 172
Tlapacoyan (Mexico), 47
Tohono O'Odham Indians
   myths of, 5–6, 11, 13–14
   reservation of, 19, 38, 63–64
"tonks," 16, 22–24, 187, 216
Tordillo Mountain, 86
towers (rescue), 213–15
trackers. *See* signcutters
Traffic (movie), 61
El Tri (band), 75
Tucson (Arizona), 9, 13, 79
   Border Patrol in, 18–20, 32, 39, 85,
      179, 214
   hospitals in, 179–81
   as illegals' destination, 64, 100, 192
   Mexican consulates in, 18, 33–38,
      207, 211, 214–15, 218–19
Twilight Zone (TV show), 154
Twin Peaks, 85

United States government
   Bureau of Labor Statistics, 217
   Bureau of Land Management, 79–80,
      173
   Customs Service, 79
   Department of Public Safety, 210
   Department of the Interior, 79
   Forest Service, 79
   Park Service, 78–79, 110
   policies of, 54–55, 76–77, 134, 204–5,
      215
   See also law enforcement agencies
University Medical Center (Tucson),
   179–80

Vargas, Rita (consul), 33, 182–84,
   186–87, 191, 195–98, 201, 204
Vásquez, Don Francisco, 61
Vazquez Landa, Irma, 146–47
Veracruz (Mexico)
   Federales in, 202
   as home of Yuma 14/Wellton 26, 39,
      92, 95, 137, 148, 182–83, 187
   life in, 43–48, 88
   return to, 191, 196–99
Veracruz Mountains, 197
Victor Rosales (Mexico), 95
Vidrios Drag, 14–16, 19, 25, 31, 56,
   180, 211

Luis Alberto Urrea is the author of *Across the Wire*, winner of the Christopher Award, and *By the Lake of Sleeping Children*. He is the recipient of an American Book Award, a Western States Book Award, and a Colorado Book Award, and he has been inducted into the Latino Literary Hall of Fame. His poetry has been included in *The Best American Poetry*, and his most recent book, *Six Kinds of Sky*, won the 2002 *ForeWord Magazine* Book of the Year Award, Editor's Choice for Fiction. He teaches creative writing at the University of Illinois at Chicago.